HOW TO BE

SANE

A GROUNDBREAKING
MENTAL WELLNESS GUIDE

DR. THERESA LAWN*

A GORGEOUS FEMALE DOCTOR

*as told to Emily Altman

Andrews McMeel
PUBLISHING®

Andrews McMeel Publishing
a division of Andrews McMeel Universal
1130 Walnut Street, Kansas City, Missouri 64106

www.andrewsmcmeel.com

23 24 25 26 27 SHO 10 9 8 7 6 5 4 3 2 1

ISBN: 978-1-5248-7375-2

Library of Congress Control Number: 2023935462

Illustrations by James Mied

Editor: Charlie Upchurch
Art Director: Holly Swayne
Production Editor: Brianna Westervelt
Production Manager: Chadd Keim

ATTENTION: SCHOOLS AND BUSINESSES
Andrews McMeel books are available at quantity discounts with bulk purchase
for educational, business, or sales promotional use. For information, please
e-mail the Andrews McMeel Publishing Special Sales Department:
sales@amuniversal.com.

To my family

CONTENTS

"I do not suffer from insanity, I enjoy every minute of it."

—Edgar Allan Poe

"Sanity is a cozy lie."

—Susan Sontag

"Whoa oh oh/ Go totally crazy
Forget I'm a lady/
Man's shirts/ Short skirts."

—Shania Twain

ON HOW TO USE THIS BOOK

Hello! If you're reading this, that means that you're looking for greater mental wellness, and I'm so very glad you're here: welcome. This book outlines all existing mental health issues, approaches them from every possible angle, and gives you the tools you need to then completely resolve them.

If you only have *some* mental health issues and not all, that's fine—you can simply flip to the chapters that are most relevant to you. But if you have them all, which you do, that's perfectly all right, and I knew it. From this therapist's point of view you're packed and you're stacked—and I look forward to guiding you on your healing journey.

If you happen to have issues that *aren't* covered in this book, let me know by emailing them to me at DrTheresaLawn@gmail.com. I'll update further editions with whatever new issue you have.[1]

Throughout the book, I'll be asking you to complete small worksheets, exercises, and games to assist in your mental recovery. I'd like to start with a small evaluation

---

[1] If it's real. Please don't flood my inbox with things like "I'm afraid of jelly beans" or "I speak to my conditioner" because that feels made up.

here, for your own purposes, so that you might better understand your own concerns and choose your own path. You can then use this survey to guide where you'd like to begin.

Good luck and let the healing . . . begin!

Dr. Theresa Lawn
December 2022, Redondo Beach

MY MENTAL HEALTH

My main issues are:

_____

_____

_____

_____

_____

One thing I worry about is:

_____

_____

_____

_____

_____

One time I felt like I could use some assistance was:

_____

_____

_____

_____

_____

Most people who are mentally healthy do _____

_____

_____

_____

_____ every day.

Three things I would like to get out of my work with Dr. Theresa Lawn:

1. _____

_____

_____

_____

2. _____

_____

_____

_____

3. _____

_____

_____

_____

Circle the best answer:

I look forward to/am worried about/am ambivalent about working with Dr. Theresa Lawn.

I understand/am trying to understand/will eventually understand that she is committed to helping me on my mental health journey.

To me mental wellness looks like:

_____

_____

_____

_____

_____

_____

_____

Okay, okay, wait, wait—Hi! Dr. Theresa Lawn again. When last we connected, you were going to do this worksheet, yes? I left you to it, ate a Lara bar, and mentally I had kind of moved on. But the more I thought about it, I got the sense—and I get senses about people—that you're just staring at it. Or worse, that you just breezed past it. This book is not an exercise in breeziness, folks!

Let's get real: You didn't do the worksheet. Are you perhaps overwhelmed? I can understand that. Maybe you were hoping someone would hold your hand a little bit more through this process, which makes total sense. You may have even thought: "I bought this book because someone had already written it, and, and—and now she's asking *me* to add more words?! That's illegal!" Okay, while I'm not sure I agree with that, I can understand how an exercise seems like a lot of work to do right up top. What if you're the kind of person who hasn't worked a day in their life! I don't *think* that's you because look at your hands . . . so maybe it's more that you're afraid? This work is not going to be easy, and honestly, what if your issue is you're scared of worksheets? We don't know. We can't know at this point. Whatever's going on with you, I think I may have gone too far too fast.

From now on, in this book I'll take a more collaborative approach. I'll give clear examples first when I ask you to do the work. I'll also tell you a little bit more about myself—who I am, why I do what I do, and why I think mental health is important. If I'm asking you to open up, well, so should I! Who am I after all—and why should you trust me?

THE DR. THERESA LAWN STORY

"I need to talk to you."

My advisor, Dr. Evans, whispered those words and gestured for me to follow him out of the psychology library. I was annoyed. I've always been a bit of a bookworm, but instead of eating apples, my "fruit" has been knowledge of the human brain. So what was Dr. Evans doing disturbing my feast?

As we walked out of the library into the hallway, I noticed other young worms walking around with their books and class schedules. One of them was actually eating an apple. I laughed—it was too perfect. "Theresa!" (Dr. Evans used my first name—I wasn't yet "Dr. Theresa Lawn.") "Theresa, you've failed your Psychology 101 exam." I don't know why he said my name twice like that. Probably some sort of psychological trick. Whatever it was, it didn't work.

"Please don't say my name twice!" I barked, allowing my mouth to hang open for emphasis. Dr. Evans looked at me, his brow crinkling with what I can only assume was respect. "Ms. Lawn, you've failed the Psychology 101 exam for the fifth time, and I'm afraid we can give you no more chances. I'm going to have to ask you to leave Redondo Beach University immediately."

Wow. Looking back at that moment now, all I can think is, "Wow." Nothing else comes to mind, it's just totally blank in my head, like a wall of ice-cold stainless steel. But . . . if I think just a little bit longer, I begin to realize something important. Yes, that dismissal devastated me at the time. But what I couldn't know was that that moment would be the moment when my true life began. Redondo Beach University let me go, but I didn't let that stop me. In fact, it fueled me. I was destined to help people. I had insights into the human brain that I needed to share. If I couldn't complete my studies at RBU, I would go elsewhere. Who needed Dr. Evans?!

And yet . . . Dr. Evans's words stayed with me. Maybe there was something to what he said: "I need to talk to you."

He needed to *talk* to me. God, what was it about talking? Why do we do it? When did it start? *Why* did it start? Why do some cultures do it, while others gave it up centuries ago?

Why are we humans *obsessed* with talking?

At this point, I knew I was onto something, so a few weeks after I left RBU, I enrolled at a different university, whose name is not important right now. What *is* important is that there I began to study not only talking but talk therapy, and how we can use dialogues and role-plays as part of the therapeutic process. At this university, whose name is irrelevant at this point, I also developed other activities—free writing, worksheets, quizzes—designed to enhance mental and emotional wellbeing through fun, creativity, and play. Who says "fun" and "therapy" have to be mutually exclusive? I think if you're doing it right, therapy should feel like you're in a bouncy castle with all of your pain, and as I tell patients all the time: You might as well jump. Go ahead . . . and jump.

After graduating from the second university (You're obsessed! It doesn't matter where! Maybe it's Yale?), I opened my own therapy practice in—you guessed it—Redondo Beach. To say I flourished would be the understatement of the last five centuries. I was just the breath of fresh air that the Redondo Beach mental health community needed, and soon I thought: Why not write a book with my insights on mental health and include in it some of my famed exercises, so that people across the globe could connect with my words and hopefully heal themselves? What you have in your mannish hands is that book. I'd say I hope it provides you with deep peace, but I'm confident enough to say I *know* that it will. Good luck <u>not</u> healing, honestly.

What I hope you've taken away from my story is my passion for investigating the human mind, and how I'll stop at nothing to help people. Now I wouldn't call myself a hero, or a shero, and definitely not a gyro.[2] However, I *do* know I have wisdom to share, and I hope learning about my path helps you to open up and trust me as we approach the work that lies ahead.

But wait . . . what of Dr. Evans, you ask? Ah. Well, I haven't seen him in many years. I hope he's alive, but he was pretty old when he was my advisor. Or at least he read as old. He may have been in his forties, but he had the vibe of someone in their late eighties, you know what I mean? He simply was not a vital man, and I felt like his days were numbered. But whether he is dead or not, his words stayed with me, and for that, I thank him.

"I need to talk to you," Dr. Evans said. Today, when you read this book, imagine me, Dr. Theresa Lawn, speaking directly to you: "I want to talk to *you*."

Good luck. You may now begin the work.

---

[2] As Tina Turner after three straight weeks of concerts in Greece once underlined so hard on her backstage rider that the pencil went through the paper: "We don't need another gyro."

WORK
AND
CAREER

*"Genius is one percent inspiration
and ninety-nine percent perspiration."*

—Thomas Edison, cut and just dripping with sweat

Work. Scientific research has shown again and again that we actually spend many hours a week at our jobs. So it should come as no surprise that work can often be a source of stress and anxiety. Many people will even dream of their work when they go to bed at night. What does that tell you? To me it says: I'd have to hear about the dream. If it's a nice dream, I'd say their work is nice. If the dream is bad, I'd say that their work is bad. If it's a sexual dream, I'd say their workplace makes them horny. This chapter works best if you think your work is bad. If your work makes you horny, just use that energy in your life; let that horny energy guide you. Lead with that energy. Horny energy is always celebrated and always appropriate.

One of my first experiences with work was my first job. I was sixteen years old and I worked at an ice cream parlor. Fun, right? Unfortunately, you're wrong. The job was a nightmare. For an entire summer I served countless happy customers, and during all that time not one of them offered me any of their ice cream. Not one soul. And we were forbidden to ask them for it! Can you imagine watching people eat ice cream all day, and not one of them extends their cone to you? None of them ever said: "Hey, you look like you would enjoy some of this! Let's share the cone—better yet, I'll work back there, you come out here and eat this cone, and then take my car." No one ever offered to take over my job and give me all of their ice cream and then their car. So I think you can see why the subject of stress at work hits very close to home for me.

One of the things that compounds this stress is that Americans in particular have the disease of defining ourselves by our work. The first thing we ask one another in a conversation is: "What do you do?" as if "what we do" is the sum total of our identity. In other parts of the world, you'd never dream of starting a conversation this way! In other cultures, work isn't considered the most interesting or important thing about a person. In France, for example, you can start a conversation by simply saying:

"Should we have a five-way?"—and just like that, you're learning something deeper and more substantive than "How do you make money?"

And it's not just France that takes this broader view of knowing one another. All of Europe seems to understand that as a person we are so much more than what we earn, or how we earn it. In Italy, for example, conversations begin when an Italian extends a noodle toward you. You bite on one end, they bite on the other, soon you are kissing, and that's amore. Did you notice how in that exchange "career" was never mentioned once? While I'm proud to be an American, sometimes I can't help but wonder if this other cultural style might be best. Less emphasis on how we pay the bills, more emphasis on who we really are.

Okay, Dr. Theresa, get off your soapbox! Sorry about that. I never mean to get political, but sometimes the political is personal. For me it was in 2004—because that was the year I dated Bob Dole, and it was very sexual. But that's another story, for another book (*On the Dole: An Unexpected Love Story*, Houghton Mifflin, 2024). *This* book is about the challenges of our daily lives, and I believe work is one of the big ones.

Now, as you head into the exercise that follows on work, remember this: Whatever job you have, it will always have its "ups and downs." This is especially true for roller coaster repairmen. The reason for that is because when roller coaster repairmen are called to work, it's usually a sad day because there's been a fatality. So it's an "up" because they're working, but it's a "down" because of the loss of life. For roller coaster repairmen, a best-case-scenario day would be: "Someone's been maimed, but they're alive, please come in and fix the car that they got maimed in." That would be a *good* day.

This chapter, and this whole book, is dedicated to roller coaster repairmen.

WORK AND CAREER

What is your dream job? In the following worksheet, I'd like you to outline exactly what your dream job consists of. What would it be like? How would it make you feel? When you've finished, reflect on your answers, and consider the ways you might be holding yourself back. What you find may surprise you. On the following page, you'll find the worksheet, which I've completed as an example. After that, you'll find a blank one for you to fill out on your own.

MY DREAM JOB

Name:

Dr. Theresa Lawn

Nicknames:

DR;TL, Lawnathan Therhys Meyers, Dr. T and the Women

Occupation:

Therapist

Dream Job:

Riding a white elephant around, and everyone seeing. Maybe the elephant is iridescent.

Do you do this now?:

No

Why do you not do this now?:

Can't phind the right 'phant

How do you imagine this job would make you feel?:

Powerful

Can you be more specific about this feeling?:

Powerful because only I do this, only I was able to find an
opalescent elephescent. Also, I have big muscles because of climbing
up on him (or her) every day, so the muscles in my butt and legs
are massive, and they communicate my power too.

Do you feel this way at your current job?:

Yeah. 'Cause my butt and legs are already super ripped. I don't
need an elephant to create the body of the future.

In what way do you think this dream job serves the world?:

People are generally bummed out because they don't smell great, and their bodies are bad, and then their skin is even worse, so at least this way they could be looking at a cool elephant for a second and be distracted from that stuff.

What is holding you back from pursuing this job?:

Fucking nothing. I've got endless courage, charisma, and know-how, I could do the elephant thing and still be Redondo Beach's leading therapeutic professional, and—look out—I might even steal ya girl while I'm at it.

What are three actual, practical steps you can take to make your dream job a reality?:

1. Find an elephant, regardless of color—we can adjust in post.

2. Pick out a saddle (Studded? Padded? Push-up?).

3. I don't know. I'm not a practical person.

WORKSHEET

MY DREAM JOB

Name:

_____
_____
_____
_____

Nicknames:

_____
_____
_____
_____

Occupation:

_____
_____
_____
_____

Dream Job:

_____
_____
_____
_____

Do you do this now?:

Why do you not do this now?:

How do you imagine this job would make you feel?

Can you be more specific about this feeling?

Do you feel this way in your current job?

In what way do you think this dream job serves the world?

_____

_____

_____

_____

What is holding you back from pursuing this job?

_____

_____

_____

_____

What are three actual, practical steps you can take to make your dream job
a reality?:

1. _____

_____

_____

2. _____

_____

_____

3. _____

_____

_____

THE FAMILY

"When you're here, you're family."

—The Holy Muslim Koran

"Family." Our psychological journeys so often begin and end with that simple word. In our sessions my clients and I address it so often and with such intensity that I like to say that "Family" is the true "F" word. You can say it again and again and it never loses its power. You could say "F--k" a million times in a book, but the truth is, we will *always* find the word "family" more powerful. Take a look at this:

1. Fuck Fuck Fuck Fuck Fuck Fuck Fuck Fuck Fuck Fuck Fuck Fuck Fuck Fuck Fuck Fuck Fuck Fuck Fuck Fuck Fuck Fuck Fuck Fuck Fuck Fuck Fuck Fuck. Fuck Fuck Fuck Fuck Jesus and Satan Fuck Fuck Fuck Fuck Fuck Fuck Fuck Fuck Fuck Fuck Fuck Fuck Fuck Fuck Fuck.

2. Family.

Now, I ask you: Which one of those statements is more shocking? It's the second, and you know that's true.

We humans have many deep, primal emotions concerning our families. Our families can provoke psychological issues, issues that take seed when we are children and remain hidden in our bodies and minds until we mature and ripen into firm, delicious adults. Over the years I've discovered that when it comes to family, what we think is personal usually turns out to be universal. I have an exercise later on that will help you discover that for yourself. But before we launch into the work at hand, let me share a small story with you that illuminates the influence that family can have over our lives.

A Romanian man named Dennis lived in Gainesville, Florida. He lived with his three lovely daughters and his Irish wife, Maureen. Dennis and Maureen ran a yogurt shop that sold delicious frozen yogurt, yogurt that came in many surprising and compelling flavors. The couple raised their daughters with all the values of their respective cultures, and as such, their daughters grew up to be half Romanian, half Irish. Because they lived in America, this wasn't a huge deal, but wherever they went in Gainesville, the children were usually the only half Romanian, half Irish people.

Looking behind the counter at the yogurt shop, customers would often smile at the happy family. "This blend of cultures—this is what all of America will look like in the future," remarked a customer one day, smiling. Dennis laughed aloud, tickled: Yogurt was a blend of active cultures . . . and so was his family! However, another customer was not smiling: "I guess I get what you mean about the blend, but I hope not 'all of America,' because that would mean there'd only be Romanian and Irish people. My family comes from the Basque region of Spain. Should we kill ourselves, according to you?"

A moment of silence. Then the two customers smiled and nodded respectfully at one another. This was America: rich in its dialogues, strengthened even in its differences.

One day, Dennis's eldest daughter Shannon said to him: "Dad, when I leave the yogurt shop one day to attend university, I will miss you and Mom so much. How will I be able to keep our traditions alive? How can I carry you all with me in my heart?" Dennis looked at her. "But daughter Shannon," he said. "You don't have the grades to get into any schools. Even a vocational school or something like that. It's not an option for you in any way. Get used to our house because I would honestly be surprised if you ever left. And that's my Romanian two cents." Shannon smiled. She sucked and wouldn't go to school after all. A father always knows.

EXERCISE

FAMILY

For this chapter, I invite you to engage with my most often used role-play exercise involving the topic of family. I have used it many times with my patients and find that it cuts to the primal truths of the relationships we have with our families of origin. When you work in the mental health sector for as long as I have, you begin to see psychological patterns emerge in your clients. In this way, patients are like a Magic Eye poster: If you study them closely enough, you might see something interesting.

If I'm being honest, I wish my patients were *more* like Magic Eye posters. One of these days I'd love to see a dolphin come out of them, or a vintage Cadillac. It's not like you can just see those things, they're only found in Magic Eye posters, so I will keep staring at my patients, my eyes boring into them, hour after hour—I only hope that eventually they will do the right thing and give me what I want.

That said, what I *have* seen emerge from my patients thus far are a number of common psychological issues, like the fact that most of their family problems stem from miscommunication. For years I've worked on a dialogue that would address this issue specifically, and on the next page, you will find that "role-play." I know it will help you reflect on, and fully solve, whatever issue it is you are having with your family. Use the template to hash out whatever it is you need—the blank spaces are for when *you* are to speak in the dialogue. The words and conflict will no doubt be deeply familiar to you, because this conflict is a conflict that is as old as time, and as universal as Universal Studios Florida. Good luck, reader—and good healing.

A CONFLICT WITH MOTHER

MOM: So does Mark Ruffalo do all the *Law and Order*s then?

YOU: _____

_____

_____

_____

MOM: Vincent D'Onofrio? No, I know who that is. He did . . . um . . . the what's it. I know who he is. He's tall.

YOU: _____

_____

_____

_____

MOM: I know he's not Vince Vaughn! I know that. Vince Vaughn was *The Swinger*.

YOU: _____

_____

_____

_____

MOM: No, wasn't that one the sequel? *Swingers*? Plural?

YOU: _____

_____

_____

_____

MOM: Well, they should've made a second one! "You're money, baby." Heather Graham . . . what happened to her? That's probably my favorite movie, you know.

YOU: _____

_____

_____

_____

MOM: Well, I <u>do</u> love it, I happen to love _Swinger_ and you don't actually know everything about your dear old mom.

YOU: _____

_____

_____

_____

MOM: _Swingers_, or _The Swinger_, or _Swing-a-Ding-a-ling_—fine! It doesn't matter what it's called! Wait, what's that on your wrist?

YOU: _____

_____

_____

_____

MOM: No no no, you show me right now you— (gasps)

YOU: _____

_____

_____

_____

MOM: You were "going" to tell me you got a tattoo? My god . . . my child is . . . an advertisement for McDonald's, why . . . why would you get the logo?! And the . . . hold on . . . is that you WITH . . . Ronald McDonald? You're in it? Why are you with him?

YOU: _____

_____

_____

_____

MOM: You're right, I don't understand! It's a fast-food restaurant, Theresa! He's a clown they use in the advertisements, you don't have a . . . a . . . *relationship* with him.

YOU: _____

_____

_____

_____

MOM: How did this happen, we barely went there, I didn't take you guys there—

YOU: (confident silence)

MOM: What are you doing to him in the tattoo?

YOU: _____

_____

_____

_____

MOM: Let me see again. Let me see!
You exit, head and wrist held high.

LOVE AND RELATIONSHIPS

"Love is what separates humans from animals.
Animals only know hate."

—Charles Darwin

L   ove. It's what we're all searching for. Humans are hardwired to seek love and affection, and yet those are often the hardest things to find. But if you are one of those who is unhappy with their romantic life, my first piece of advice to you is this: You mustn't spend your whole life thinking about what you <u>don't</u> have. Countless psychological studies have shown this kind of thinking only makes things worse. Don't make the mistake of thinking: "But only when I have a partner will I be happy, only *then* will I be whole!" Dear reader, you're whole already. You're not broken, you don't need to be put back together—you're not Humpty Dumpty! Humpty Dumpty sat on a wall all those centuries ago, and he fell and died, but what we so often forget is that He died so that we could *live*. So let's enjoy this life we've been given! Let's enjoy it in His name. And that means enjoying life—even if you're single, even if you're unlucky in love.[3]

Okay, but is it really that easy? You're saying it's easy, but I'm not sure I agree. In fact, the therapeutic work I've done with my patients tells me that it can be very painful, this struggle to find love. But what I'm here to tell you is that I believe there is concrete psychological work you can do to help ease this pain. I'm guessing that for many of you, this chapter was the reason you purchased the book, and I get that! You go into the bookstore, lonely, looking for answers, you pick up this book, you see the author photo— Well, well, well. Written by a cutie. Interesting. That doesn't hurt. Spring in your step: achieved.

---

[3]   Also, I just want to say Humpty wasn't supposed to play on the wall like that. In the Medieval Egg Community, you would know that's crossing a line, and Humpty knew, deep in his shell. But he *did it anyway*. He took a risk to try and find joy, even if it left him broken and in pieces. And is that so different than what we humans need to do to find love? (I'm literally asking; I don't know the answer.)

Well, I've got good news and bad news. The good news is you picking up the book was your first step toward healing. The bad news?

I'm not single.

Reader, oh NO, oh no you don't, no no no no, we don't throw books here! No. I know you're upset, but this book costs more than you make in a year, please treat it with respect. Now go and pick it up. Okay, there you go, lift with your legs, not your back, thank you. Now. Why don't you take a deep breath, and let's talk.

Okay. So yes, it's true: I'm taken. I'm dating a muscle man I met in Venice Beach, California, a man by the name of Vance Jeremy. VJ is an incredible person who just happens to have won the "Sun Buns West" invitational five years running, and he makes me whole.

Now I imagine that's no comfort to you, since you're still thinking about what could have been: "But the picture was the whole reason I bought the damn thing! I never read no fancy books before, but she's the prettiest ladyfolk I ever did see, and, and—"

And what? Come on, you must have known on some level it wouldn't work. I'm not trying to be harsh, I certainly understand how powerful your attraction must be, but at the same time, what were you thinking? Did you think reading the book would count as a date? It doesn't, because you didn't buy me anything.

Look, I said I'm sorry. Let's move on, let's stop, you're upsetting me, how stressful, oh dear, oh god—ohhhh phew. Oh, thank god. Reader, I was stressed there for a second, but just now Vance Jeremy came over and gave me a shoulder massage! Oh my god, *yes*. My muscles were tense from the aggression you launched at me, but all that melted away when VJ used his "magic hands." I call them his "magic hands" because he always wears Mickey Mouse–style magician's gloves. He's always oiled, his buns are high and thoroughly sunned, and he's got the gloves on. That's VJ. You're welcome for the mental picture. Is it hot in here?

Phew! Well, now that VJ's gone back to his chamber, I guess let's get back to you, reader. You're clearly still upset. But seriously, what could I have done to prevent this? Perhaps I should've just worn a walrus suit in my author photo, maybe that would help ease some potential heartbreak. Hmm, yeah . . . but on the other hand, then people might find themselves falling for the most gorgeous walrus they've ever seen, a walrus with soulful eyes, perfect skin, and tusks that go all the way around.

And . . . now you're all worked up again. Sorry. Forget that sexy walrus! She's unavailable. She's been shot, okay? She lies dead. Does that help?

Bit of an awkward start. However, I do hope you can already see how you're healing and learning. All of us have areas where we can grow and mature, and clearly this is a big one for you. I advise you to really spend some time on the following exercise on love and relationships. I think it will be quite useful to you, and in it you may even find resolutions to some of your weirder issues, like with the walrus. She's dead. Let it go.

LOVE AND RELATIONSHIPS

Drawing is a way to let our subconscious express itself. We do it all the time when we are young, but as adults, we tend to forget how therapeutic and illuminating the visual arts can be. When we draw, our thoughts and feelings become images, and those images tell the story of our minds. For this exercise, I'd like you think about love and relationships, and then I want you to free draw whatever comes to mind. Do not censor yourself.

Have you ever heard of Vincent Van Gogh? Well, he was a drawer who lived over one hundred years ago, and even though he had mental problems, drawing things like flowers, chairs, and old men helped him to heal entirely. Want to know more about Vincent Van Gogh? He has a drawing called *Starry Nights*, and it's said to be very beautiful. Those are the only facts we have available to us at this time about Vincent Van Gogh.

So, therefore: draw, draw, draw! There's no right way to do this, although on the following page I'll include what I drew when thinking about relationships, just as a guide, so you know the perfect way to do it. I'm just saying—then you can do it any way you want, but how cool that you'll also get to see the perfect way first.

LOVE AND RELATIONSHIPS

Dontcha wish your girlfriend was a walrus like me?

FREE DRAWING EXERCISE

LOVE AND RELATIONSHIPS

HONESTY

"Sorry, I cannot tell a lie."

—George Washington, telling Thomas Jefferson he smells like shit

Honesty is one of the most important qualities in a person. Those who are psychologically healthy live their lives with honesty and authenticity, which is why it is so important for the work we are doing in this book. Do you think you can push yourself to be truly honest? You must, if you want to be truly whole.

The only exception to this is you have a partner, because then that's also a way to be made whole. (Shout out to Vance Jeremy, whose buns have reached a tawny caramel hue. Yes, babe! A third of the way there!)

Now, am I going to sit here and pretend that I've always been 100% honest? No, because I don't have to pretend; I'm telling the truth. I've never lied, and I don't get why people would.

Question for you: Why would I lie, when the truth is so beautiful? For instance, as many of you know, I invented donut holes (I came up with the idea, invented eating them, etc.). Now I *could* lie and say: "I *also* invented rocks!" or "I made up math!" but I didn't do those things, just donut holes, and I think that's enough. Is *that* why people lie? Their own insecurity? Because they don't think the truth is "enough"? I think when we truly value ourselves, we don't need to make stuff up. I made the donut holes "up"—meaning I created them out of my imagination, and made them real, sweet, and delicious—and that is enough for me. Why fib?

Probably the best lesson I ever learned about honesty came from my blood relative and first cousin, Carlos Santana. Carlos and I are cousins, but our relationship is more like a combination of twin/best friend/soulmate. You cannot be closer to another human being than I am to Carlos Santana. Carlos calls me every day when he wakes up, twelve times throughout the day, and one final time at night before he falls asleep.

Anyways, during one of these nighttime calls, I mentioned something to him that had been weighing on me. I said to him, "'Los? You know your song 'Maria, Maria'? I love it, but it hurts my feelings." Then I wanted to move on: I didn't want to make a big thing out of it, because I'm naturally quite giving. But Carlos insisted I continue. So I took a big breath, and then I chose honesty. I said, "Okay, well there's that part in the song where there's the guitar solo, but before it starts, the singer guy goes, 'To the sound of the guitar . . . played by Carlos Santana.' Can you understand why that part hurts my feelings?"

There was a long pause. Finally, when Carlos Santana spoke, his voice was choked with emotion, "Of course, Theresa—you played guitar on that song, not me. I am so very sorry. There were a lot of people around I was trying to impress, and I'm weak, so I didn't correct him when he sang that line, and it actually should go, 'to the sound of the guitar, played by Dr. Theresa Lawn.' I am so very sorry."

I told him that was all well and good, but that, no, I didn't think I could ever "accept" his apology. I don't talk to him anymore. We're <u>not</u> close. We'll see each other with the rest of our family at our family reunions, but I don't let him approach me. Surely, you get it.

You get it. Right?

I feel like you're acting like that didn't happen, like I'm being crazy or something, but hello, did you read? He stole my solo! It happened, and I didn't even tell you that then I sued his ass, the case went all the way to the United States Supreme Court, they fucking ruled in my favor, they made a movie out of it, Hailee Steinfeld played me, Jaden Smith played the judge, and The Chainsmokers wrote a song that played over the credits called "American Justice (Let Freedom Ring)," and I did the guitar solo in *that* too, and I got paid one hundred million dollars for it, and there is nothing more powerful than the truth!

<u>Nothing</u>.

HONESTY

When you're accustomed to being less than honest, it can be scary to reveal the truth. When we're honest, we are our truest selves, but so often we spend our lives hiding—hiding our feelings, hiding our emotions, and hiding who we really are. But that's no way to live.

It's time to stop the secrecy, to stop the lies. Can you do that? Can you try radical honesty? In this chapter's exercise I'm going to ask you to do that, because it's time for you **to reveal to me where you have hidden your treasure**. I know you have one, it's time for me to have it now, and that's honesty.

If drawing a map is part of your honesty process, that's okay. But be explicit on the map. Don't just write "walk five paces past the old oak" because *which* oak. They all seem old. Now is the time for true transparency so include a legend. But also, is there a reason it has to be a map? If it's a cultural thing—I know for some groups, maps are traditional—okay. But if you're *not* Pirate-American, and your treasure isn't "booty," why not drop me a pin or write out Google Maps directions on the next page. How honest would that be? Wow. This is going to be so good; I just got chills for you. You've probably been hiding this treasure for years. No more hiding. No more suffering. You can release it. Honesty is so liberating!

Do you know offhand if it's all together in a trunk, or is it more like loose jewels and coins? Ideally it's more like rubies and doubloons and less like strings of pearls, just because those aren't worth as much. But it seems like usually treasure chests are draped in pearl necklaces and if that's standard, or it just comes that way, that's cool. I would imagine there's not high-end soaps in there? If you could add some, I'd love it. I'd love it. Just for guidance I tend to like soaps that smell good and look like other things, like shells or restaurant clowns.

Oh also, and this is a big one—just tell me straight if I'm going to find a skeleton with your treasure. I need your honesty on this. I can handle it, I've been working on that a lot. If I see a skeleton with your treasure, I'll take a deep breath and I'll remember that *he's* dead, I'm not, and he's not gonna get up and dance. Because the thing is, I know I'd really lose it if he got up and danced. I'd flip out, I'd throw up, I'd shit myself, the whole nine. So that's why your honesty means everything. Tell me if there's a skeleton, and if by chance he's enchanted and he likes to move, you must mention that too.

I am ready for your honesty. The question is . . . are you? Let's see. Good luck.

Where I Have Hidden My Treasure:

McDONALD'S

"Ba Da Da Da Da—I don't care for it."

—McDonald's Jingle, Early Version

McDonald's. It's often been said that aside from temples, churches, and mosques, the only true American place of worship is McDonald's. Our connection with McDonald's starts the moment we're born, and it lasts our whole lives—and some would say even beyond that. We live, eat, laugh, and love in McDonald's. We have our birthday parties there, our dates, our weddings . . . and even our funerals. And while, yes, it's always awkward to walk into a McDonald's that's having a funeral, it's also humbling. That will be you one day, in that casket. Be present when the circle of life shows itself to you. Take it in. You mustn't shy away from a man in an open casket in a McDonald's. You must look, because that man is you, that man is me—that man is all of us.

McDonald's means so much to us, on such a deep level, it's no wonder it's the center of many of our psychological issues. Hell, we have such affection for the place that sometimes we call it by a nickname. Most people, when they do this, call it "Mickey D's." A few people might call it "McDoh-Dohs." No one has ever used the nickname "Mark Donald Restaurant"—until now. And while I'm pleased I came up with something new, I'm not feeling it entirely. You're free to use it if you'd like.

What's your earliest McDonald's memory? The exercise in this chapter will touch on all the ways that McDonald's lives within us, around us, and among us. So think back, if you will, to your first McDonald's recollection. Was it going to McDonald's with your parents? Was it spilling your sweet and sour sauce on a veteran and feeling shame? Or was it something personal? Was McDonald's the first person you kissed? Now some might say that one doesn't make sense, but I would argue it does, because I think McDonald's is a person. I view McDonald's as a person, I treat McDonald's as a person, and, to me, McDonald's has the same importance as a person.

So as you complete the following McExercise, remember this: It doesn't matter whether you're a "spend ten hours a day in a McDonald's" kind of person or a "spend ten hours a week in a McDonald's" kind of person—there's something in there for all of us. Good luck.

McDONALD'S

When we think about McDonald's, what is it that we think about? What do we feel? For the following exercise, I'd like you to express your thoughts about McDonald's in clear, simple words. Don't say what you *think* you're supposed to say about McDonald's. This isn't a college class, or a church sermon, or Santa's wake—there's no "right thing" to say here. For the purposes of this exercise, my only requirement for you is that you speak from the heart and only use **words that are menu items from McDonald's or characters from the McDonaldland Universe**. No other words. The only words that matter are words that have to do with McDonald's. Use those. Any other words are horseshit. And you know the deal with horseshit, right?

It. Stinks.

Do you "fry" (see) what I "Oreo McFlurry" (mean)?

Yeah, I think you "Filet-O-Fish" (no translation).

I will give you a prompt to begin the exercise. Oh, one more thing—I hesitate to even say this, but please don't describe the McDonaldland characters having sex with one another. Don't involve the menu items either, and don't describe a pleasure palace where all the characters and menu items live together, and they just fulfill each other sexually constantly, and then Grimace comes in and— Please just stop, and please don't write anything *like* that, because it's been done. Done to death. That story has been told a million times, and usually very well, by writers (I'm sorry) far better than you. Best, again, to stay in your lane. Good luck.

What McDonald's Means to Me

Egg Mc . . .

Reader's Progress: Check-In #1

How are you doing?

_____

_____

_____

What do you think of Dr. Theresa Lawn?

_____

_____

_____

(Circle one) While I don't know her well yet, the impression I get of Dr. Theresa Lawn is: **wise but down-to-earth/brilliant but remote/beautiful but she doesn't know it/beefy**

If Dr. Theresa Lawn needed a favor from you at this point, how far would you go?

    A. Honestly? Would kill for her.

    B. Would kill for her, but softly weep after.

    C. Would push a button to kill someone for her but not actively do it/Would pay for assassination assistance, etc.

    D. I'm selfish, so I probably would just prefer to eat Cheetos in my bean bag chair, sweating, because I sweat when I eat my Cheetos in my BeanBaCha because that's where I'm at, physically.

They say women can't have it all . . . But then there's Dr. Theresa Lawn. Explain the dichotomy:

_____

_____

_____

_____

CHANGE

*"A leopard cannot change his spots.
He will always be in leopard print, and this is
what gives him his slutty appearance."*

—Sir David Attenborough

C hange. Like death, taxes, and nail art, it's just one of those parts of life that's never going away. So learning to live with change is one of life's most important lessons.

Now, when I say change, I'm not talking about that metal stuff jangling in your pocket. Nor am I talking about how you "change" your baby's diaper. I'm not even talking about the chunky, metallic string-thing that helps make the bike move. That is a chain—and I said change. Change is something different.

Change is when something that was one way in our lives becomes something different. Sometimes this "change" can be quite difficult. A good example of such a change would be your partner leaving you, because he doesn't think you should consider McDonald's a person. He says, "You've changed," and something's not right. Now, your first impulse might be to resist this change. "No, don't go!" you might cry. But what good does that do?! There's nothing wrong with your beliefs—they're perfect beliefs. If he can't accept them, well, maybe it was right for him to move on. While you didn't anticipate this change happening, if you look at it from a new perspective, it's probably all for the best. More time for you at McDoh-Dohs.

As you can see, much of approaching change and transitions is about perspective. The more you can allow life's transitions to happen, the more you can "go with the flow," the happier you will be. And if you use the power of perspective, you might see how the change opens new doors for you in your life.

Now, for a moment, I'd like you to think back to the parable of Dennis, the beloved Romanian-American patriarch we met in the chapter on family. I have another story about Dennis, one that can help us understand how change is not to be feared. In Dennis's case, you'll see that change is actually what helps bring him happiness.

One day, in middle-age, Dennis looked around at all he had accomplished. He had a beautiful Irish wife, Maureen, and their bond was strong and true. He had three lovely daughters that sucked, and they worked alongside him in the yogurt shop, where business was brisk. Marriage, family, a booming career—for most people, that would be more than enough. But in spite of all this, Dennis felt empty.

"Maureen," Dennis said. "I feel empty. But everything is good in our lives. Why is this?"

Maureen looked at Dennis. Her eyes were smiling, because Irish eyes . . . well, that's their thing. Can't turn 'em off. But what came out of Maureen's mouth next was quite serious.

"Dennis, perhaps you need to change something if you want to feel happier. While our lives are rich and full, we must continue to grow and evolve if we want to stay engaged with the world around us."

"Oh, like *you* do that!" Dennis snapped, rolling his eyes dramatically and weirdly slowly.

Maureen nodded. "I see you are troubled. I wish you luck."

Maureen left and went down to the basement. She had a whole setup down there, with a pull-down TV screen and a recliner. She logged into Hulu, scrolled through movies, and selected *Hitch*. She sat down and really fucking chilled. Dennis wasn't going to ruin her day.

Upstairs, Dennis thought about his wife's advice. Perhaps Maureen was right about this "change." But what kind of change? He would have to think. Day and night, Dennis thought of change. Finally, after seven days and three nights of thinking, he knew what he had to do.

Dennis left their home in Gainesville at dawn and drove to Cocoa Beach. In Cocoa Beach, there's a kind of promenade/boardwalk area with a Dippin' Dots; there's funnel cake, and you can get things airbrushed. Dennis walked past all those amusements and into a tattoo parlor called CocoTats. He cleared his throat and looked at the man behind the counter.

"I would like a large tribal tattoo around my upper arm. I want it to look like barbed wire, but in the wire design I want you to write my wife's name, and my daughters' names, and somewhere hidden in there, I want you to also write the word 'yogurt.'"

Dennis got the tattoo.

Dennis made a change.

Dennis . . . was happy.[4]

---

[4]   Dennis died by assisted suicide in 2009. He was still happy about all the change stuff, and his life, and all that—death was just the right move for him at that time.

CHANGE

Are you afraid of change? Why? Do you think change is Freddy Krueger, coming for you with his famously sharp fingers? Or is change Chucky from *Child's Play*, "the rude doll in the overalls," insulting you right to your face? No, no, come now, change is neither one of those things. Change is just a word, you must embrace it, and that's what this chapter's exercise will help you do.

But how does one embrace change? It's a good question. For instance, embracing change is quite different from the way I embrace my lovers. When I do that, I hold my lovers tightly, but at the same time, I'm squeezing my own buttcheeks together. I may have mentioned how strong my buttcheeks are? My whole butt structure is: the cheeks, the muscles, and the bones. So flexing all of this while hugging people gives me a profound sense of honor and pride. Of course, that embrace is innovative and powerful, but what I'm saying is that's *not* the way we embrace change.

Well, actually, you *can* squeeze your buttcheeks together as you're embracing change, but I'm just saying there also has to be an element of you addressing the change itself, whatever that is. The only way that squeezing your buttcheeks together would count as "embracing change" is if your signature thing was leaving your buttcheeks very open, and you were super committed to that lifestyle and were scared to deviate from that. Then squeezing your buttcheeks together would be embracing change.

Do you understand it yet? Are you ready to embrace change? In this chapter's exercise, I invite you to embrace change by reaching deep inside yourself and engaging with the very core of your essence, bravely choosing to see yourself in a new way by . . . **getting bangs**. This is a different kind of exercise because it requires you to put the book down and engage with the world. But moving will do you good. *Bangs* will do you good, because of your forehead, which I'm not saying there's anything wrong with, at all, but why question whether your forehead is "normal" or not when we can just tuck away the body part in question behind a curtain of your own genetic material. The debates, the curiosity, the controversy—that can all stop. Let's put the forehead question to bed right now.

Getting bangs is a simple, clear way of telling yourself and the world that you're not afraid of change, and in fact, you embrace it, and we can tell, because now there are shorter pieces of hair across your forehead. Whether you get swoopy bangs, baby bangs, or She Bangs is up to you—and all you need to do to achieve this is put down the book, go outside of your foul-smelling hut, and get yourself to a Supercuts.

"But Dr. T, I'm scared!"

Hey there, I know you are, but let me tell you something: Haircuts don't hurt. Hair is mostly numb; you can barely feel it when they cut it. It's more like one quick pinch and then your whole body goes ice-cold and then white-hot, and then you can't see for the remainder of the calendar year. After that, you're done, and that's all. You can do this. You're going to go out and get bangs and embrace change.[5] I'm proud of you.

---

[5] If you already have bangs, then great. *Your* assignment is to tell people you "just got bangs today" and let *them* feel like the crazy ones for once.

MONEY

"Money can *buy you Happiness."*

—Me handing over my DVD copy of Todd Solondz's *Happiness* to the guy
I'm selling it to[6]

---

[6] Now I have money to go buy drugs! Yes!!!! I am *addicted* to drugs—I seriously cannot get enough.

When people think of money, many view it as simply a fact of life—not something that would come up in relation to their mental health, let alone in their therapeutic work. But those "many" are wrong. In my sessions, almost every client must at some point confront their psychological relationship to money, a relationship that often stems from childhood, upbringing, or family of origin. Money isn't just what we use to pay the bills—money can mean status, safety, security, and even identity. Because of this, sadly, some people spend their entire lives solely focused on acquiring money—and never even entertain an alternative value system.

But I ask you this: What if you didn't *have* to spend your whole life as a slave to the "almighty dollar"? What if you drew joy and fulfillment from all the things in life that are meaningful, things besides money? At the end of the day, life isn't about how many dollars are in your bank account or how much money you made last year. Life isn't about money, dear reader. Life is about *things*: property, art, jewelry, cars, emeralds, and high-end soaps. This is what life is about, so being obsessed with *money* is just about the dumbest thing in the world. Money is paper and round metal things, and honestly, if you're so into that, literally go through any trash can and you'll find that stuff.

Why am I getting the sense though that you'd actually do that? You'd probably find some green scraps and an old bottle cap and clap your hands together, drooling, like: "Yay yay money time for me, doody farts." Well, I'm really sorry, but that's not the kind of life I want to live. I'm looking for something much bigger than money. I want a fancy car, and I want a lot of jewelry—and I want the jewelry to be fancy too. I want many houses, and I don't really care where—because it's not about the *location*, it's about the feeling of owning stuff.

And, by the way, it's not all "stuff" either, or objects—because I want horses too. I want a horse farm, an ostrich farm, an alpaca farm, and a chinchilla farm—and I want to hire someone to teach me the difference between all those creatures. Life isn't "all about the Benjamins"; it's "all about getting the max amount of elite and exotic animals."

You probably wouldn't want an animal farm, though. Or any farm, unless it's, like, a money farm. Cool! Go ahead, live in a farmhouse made out of paper and, like, watch paper and metal blow around or something? Meanwhile, I'm going to be opening my own water park, a private one, just for me, directly next to an already existing water park, and however tall their slides are, mine are gonna be just a little taller, and the slides faster and longer, and I'm going to angle my whole park to face their park, so the people there have to see what I have, and how it's all mine, and how it's the best.

My ultimate dream—and I feel a little shy sharing this part, but okay—my ultimate dream would be . . . to run the other water park out of business because people feel so bummed seeing what they have isn't that great, so they stop going. Now, I know that dream sounds wild. But if you're going to dream, dream big. Don't just dream about kissing a dollar bill while putting coins in your butt, I guess, like it's a fucking coin purse. Those are *your* dreams.

MONEY

Now that we've talked a bit about money and its value to us, it's time to take a critical look at the actual role of real money that we have in our lives. How are we using our money? What do the things we acquire say about us? On the following pages, I'd like you to write out one day's spending, then take some time to think about how the items you've bought reflect upon your identity, your values, and your place in your community. We often spend mindlessly, but this exercise should begin to give you clarity and perspective on what your money means to you. As an example, to give you that framework that you crave, I am including my own spending from Monday. Good luck!

DR. THERESA LAWN

Avocado Toast $12

Iced Latte $5

Hot Latte $7

Avocado Bruschetta $5

Latte $5

Custom Latte Art (of Avocado Toast) $8

McLatte $4

Ronald McAvocadonald's Toast $5

Tepid Latte $5

Bad Latte $5

Toasted Rustic Bread with Avocado Crème $18

2 Tickets to "The Atties" (The Avocado Toast Awards) hosted by
    Christine Lahti (pronounced "latte") $900

Guacamole on Bread $8

Avocado Spice Latte $6

Pornographic Magazines $1,331.58

Total: Priceless

YESTERDAY'S SPENDING

YOU

CHILDREN

"When I was a child, I spoke as a child, I understood as a child, I thought as a child. But when I became a man, I put away childish things . . .
and took out my man things: Head and Shoulders 2-in-1 Anti Dandruff and a jock strap."

—The Bible

What is a child? Well, you were a child, I was a child: Everyone was a child once. In order to know ourselves, and do the real, true, deep work of healing, we must go back and get in touch with who we were as children. Childhood is when we absorb our first joys and our first traumas, things that create the foundation for who we are to become psychologically as adults. It's often been said that the way we relate to children is also the way we relate to our own younger selves. In psychology, we call this younger self the "inner child."

But what exactly is an inner child? Inner children are so common, sometimes you're seeing an inner child and you don't even know it. For instance, did you know the movie *Alien* was about when someone's inner child busted out of them? That's true, and what the film teaches us is that you must love your inner child, or it will destroy you.

And yet . . . some of us still struggle with loving our inner children because we are carrying childhood shame. This is shame that we must let go of; shame from when we stole a cookie from Granny's cookie jar, or when we broke sister Tina's baby doll, or when we hit a baseball right through the window of Old Man Thompson's house and it hit him squarely between the eyes and he was killed instantly. When we think of these moments, we shudder with shame, because those inner children are still inside of us, carrying their regret. We need to forgive ourselves, because if we hold on to shame, it will kill us, like Old Man Thompson, and also Mrs. Thompson, who we shot when she saw what we had done and was about to call the police. The question is: Can we forgive the child inside of us? We <u>can</u>, through connecting with children now, as adults. But how can *I* connect with a child, you ask? The role-play exercise that follows this chapter will tell you exactly how to do this.

"Dr. T, I don't know about this role-play. I don't know what I would even *say* to a small one!"

It's okay. First of all, don't call them "a small one." Where did you get that? Did you mean "little one"? They're going to know you're a cop if you say "small one." By the way, you're a cop, right? I want you to be. I meant to mention that at the beginning. My dream is that this book is a cops-only zone. Love your hats, your outfits, love everything about you guys. If you're not a cop and reading this, that's . . . okay, I guess, just promise me you'll go to a police academy and rise through the ranks and eventually become a lieutenant. Otherwise, I think you should stop reading because this book isn't for you.

Or actually, wait, wait, wait— If you're already a cop, that's great, like I said, this book is for you, and I'm <u>not</u> worried about what I just said about Old Man Thompson or Mrs. Thompson! It doesn't stress me out that you know about that. I'm not worried, because this book is a *fantasy* book, and you know that; it was in the fantasy book section and it's kind of like *Game of Thrones*, like, it's supposed to be next to those books, so that was a *fantasy* what I said back there about the Thompson family and their deaths. If you thought it was real . . . I guess the book was misshelved or something? Because this book is a fantasy book about a British family who take their castle and turn it into an Airbnb for dragons. Basically, all of the fantasy of the book comes out of that situation: the Airbnb, the dragons that are coming and going, how they get the keys, etc. . . . so . . . you know what, I actually *don't* think that kind of material is something that you cops will actually get and . . . I'm sorry, maybe this book isn't for cops. Sorry about that. Goodbye, cops.

Have the cops left? Phew! I hate to watch bacon go, but I love the smell of it as it leaves, know what I mean? Anyways . . . where were we? What is a child? Did we ever answer that question? I can't remember, and unfortunately, I can't go back; I need to always move forward or I will die, like a shark whose boss is holding a gun to his head. But I *believe* we were talking about children, how to connect with them, and your upcoming role-play exercise. So now it's time to give it a try. You'll get a chance to practice connecting with a child, so have fun, be kind, and really get to know them. Let this bond you have with a child help you to forgive and heal your own inner child. She did nothing wrong. Good luck, and I hope you find it enriching . . .

. . . kid. ;)

CONNECTING WITH CHILDREN

YOU: _____
_____
_____
_____

CHILD: No, my mom's just right there in the bathroom. (*Points to bathroom door*) We're leaving.

YOU: _____
_____
_____
_____

CHILD: Not really, thank you. I have my book. (*Opens book*)

YOU: _____
_____
_____
_____

CHILD: Sorry, I'm fifteen, I don't really "play"—Mom? (*knocks on bathroom door*)

YOU: (*revealing something from your bag*) _____
_____
_____
_____

CHILD: Yeah, okay, I see you have a banana.

YOU: _____

_____

_____

_____

CHILD: Yeah, no, I get it, you're using it like a phone. (_Pushing away banana)_ No, I don't want it, thank you.

YOU: _____

_____

_____

_____

 CHILD: Yeah, no, there's no "monkey I want to call"—(_knocks on door_) Mom, hurry up!

YOU: _____

_____

_____

_____

CHILD: No, my mom and I are—are just leaving, don't know why she's taking so—

YOU: (_pulling out something else from your bag_) _____

_____

_____

_____

CHILD: Yeah, an iPhone. Cool.

YOU: _____

_____

_____

_____

CHILD: Yeah, I get it, you've got the "banana phone" *and* the iPhone. Cool, both, okay, yup, now you're making like the iPhone's the banana, okay, you're peeling it, you're a monkey, yup, you're—

YOU: (*Garbled mouth sounds*)

CHILD: MOM! MOM!! (*Banging on door*) This lady just *ate* her iPhone, MOM!— (*Mom runs out of bathroom*) She ate her iPhone, she said it was for me, I didn't ask her to do it, I don't—

Congratulations. Bringing a smile to a child's face is the very definition of class.

POLITICS
AND
MODERN
AMERICA

"Never discuss politics on a first date; don't discuss anything.
You must never speak, but DO make air puff out of your nostrils
to let your man know you're having a good time."

—*Cosmopolitan* Magazine, May 2016

What do politics have to do with mental health? Well, I've said this, but the political is personal and if you don't know that . . . you're mentally unhealthy and should be chemically castrated.

Whoa, whoa, *whoa* there! *Chemically castrated*!? Hey, that's kind of an extreme point of view! Well, it *is* extreme, and I only say it to show you how upsetting, mentally and emotionally, it can be to confront viewpoints different from your own. And that's what it is to talk about politics.

Politics are *very* personal. Now, you might remember that the slogan for the film *Jaws 2* was: "This time, it's personal." Well, as I always say to everyone I've ever met: That slogan *should* have been, "This time, it's politics," because that means the same thing. I also think that then, on the poster, you could have had Jaws the Shark in an Uncle Sam hat! Another thought coming to me now is, while I know the shark is supposed to be scary, what if you took the shark out, and the whole movie was just people having sex with each other? There could be close ups, you see every part of their bodies, it's sex, they're really having it, and that's the whole movie. If you want to still call it *Jaws 2*, okay . . . but why? We all know that the movies that stay with us the most, the ones that we truly love, the ones we end up watching again and again—those are all movies where it's just people having sex with each other. So why not make more of those? Those movies are the heartbeat of America. And *that's* today's Chevrolet.

Do you agree with all that I just said? Or are you challenged by my beliefs? Did I confuse you? I imagine your mind is reeling. If that's the case, let's discuss how you might better approach dealing with opposing points of view, political or otherwise. I'll now share with you the times I've been confronted with political points of view different from my own, and how I've not only managed to hold my own—I've triumphed.

Like most of you, I have been confronted by the Venice Beach Police on over thirty-seven separate occasions, and I'm sure you can already guess the reason: politics. What's funny is they'll give you every reason in the book *except* that one, but that's all it is. Oh, they'll point the finger at you, because they need someone to take the blame, but all it's ever about is keeping the greedy fatcats down at City Hall happy, or paying off whatever lobbyist is kissing their ass that week. Fortunately for me, I know how to play the game, and now so will you. Here's a sampling of three times I've <u>owned</u> the VBPD, when they tried to make my "personal" . . . "political." Pay close attention.

Example 1:
(*Siren sound*) Officer: "Ma'am, the muscle men saw you looking through the hole into their locker room, you can't do that."

Me: (*Mocks siren sound*) "Oh, please. Who's running for reelection? Leave me alone with that Beltway insider bullshit."

Example 2:
Officer: "Ma'am, we've told you before, the muscle men can and will self-oil. They ask that you do not attempt to oil them or offer assistance."

Me: "Wow, seems you get really concerned about conflicts when *oil* is involved. What's that about? (*cough*) Dollar signs (*cough*) corporate greed. Didn't see you when the muscle men were *dry*. That's when I was snapping their speedos, you know."

Officer: "We know, we were here, we stopped you and told you you can't do that, and you said that you had (*checks notes*) 'crazy hands disease' where your 'hands are mentally ill and you have paperwork, it's in your car, and you can park in handicapped spots because of it.'"

Me: (*Does stuff with hands*)

Example 3:

Officer: "Ms. Lawn, The Bunmen have united to file a formal restraining order against you. They are not afraid for their safety but agree that it might be best for *your* well-being. You are not allowed in any of the event tents or merch tables for SunBuns West 2019. Now please leave."

A Voice: "Wait!"

(*Squeaking and sliding sounds as an extremely greasy man sprints from the locker room toward me, slipping twelve different times before arriving at my side.*)

Vance Jeremy: "Take me with you." (*Slips*)

Me: (*winks*) "My my my, aren't you an oily one. Can I call you . . . Mr. Grease—"

Officer: "Ma'am, we've asked you to leave—"

Me: (*Revs engine angrily, rears dune buggy on back wheels as VJ slides aboard, honks horn, which plays "Linger" by the Cranberries, drives buggy directly into the ocean*)

After all of that, not everyone would remember that the theme of this chapter is politics. But *you* do, because now you're remembering that the *political* is *personal*, and I shared a very personal story with you. If our country is going to come together, we cannot let politics divide us. We can't shy away when we have an actual chance to debate one another, a chance for connection, a chance for understanding. You must have these political conversations while hopefully feeling strong, grounded, and sane throughout. So what will you do? On the next page, you'll find a quiz that will help determine what level of civic responsibility is right for you, and how you can achieve it while maintaining your fragile mental health. You're not well, but I care for you. Good luck.

POLITICS, AMERICA, AND ME

What is your current relationship to politics? Are you able to engage with the civic and political world with relative ease, or could you use some encouragement and assistance? What level of engagement is right for you, and are you able to stay mentally healthy as you do so? Answer each question in the following quiz, and at the end, tally your answers to find an accurate assessment of your situation.

1. **Did you vote in the last presidential election?**
   A. No. I'll only vote when it's God for president, Jesus Christ for VP, and the Holy Ghost for either Secretary of the Interior or Secretary of Transportation.
   B. Yes.
   C. No. I'm purple and fat and they won't let me.
   D. Nope. I don't do dumb shit.

2. **Finish the following sentence: "Oh beautiful, for spacious skies, for amber waves of _____."**
   A. Communion wafers.
   B. Grain.
   C. Fries. I hope! But they won't let me eat them because of my size.
   D. Not doing this. Grow up.

3. **One thing I wish was different in our modern American society:**
   A. CVS should sell communion wafers for when you just get a craving.
   B. Healthcare. It shouldn't be so hard to get a penis implant.
   C. Healthcare. It shouldn't be so hard to replace your testicles if you feel like it.
   D. "One thing I wish was different in our modern American society"— I DON'T CARE.

4. If someone disagrees with your political opinion, what do you do?

A. Pour myself a tall glass of communion wine, crack open a sleeve of communion wafers, and I let go and let God. It's not for me to judge, and if they're really wrong, God will give them diarrhea anyway.[7]

B. Shrug my shoulders and get another penis implant.

C. Slink back to my home, which is a purple nest underneath every McDonald's.

D. I'm not gonna tell you. You want to be me so bad.

5. And finally: Who is the Greatest American Who Ever Lived?

A. God. Just wish he'd share his COMMUNION WAFER RECIPE!!! Y'all can keep your "chocolate chip cookies"—<u>God</u> made a cookie called communion wafers, that's what *I* eat. ♪♪ "CC" is for CHRIST'S COOKIES/ that's good enough for me! ♪♪

B. Dr. Theresa Lawn.

C. Mayor McCheese. Even though we disagreed on some things (he believed in the death penalty for all crimes), I still respected him for having a hat, wearing a sash, and making it all look gay. He was gay, he was Irish-American, he was a mayor. He died of unnatural causes in 2002.

D. Eat shit.

---

[7] BTW home remedy for diarrhea—take two communion wafers and call me in the morning (to thank me!).

RESULTS:

1. *If your answers are mostly As*—Congratulations. You seem really removed from politics, because you're deeply religious, in a new, weird way—seems like it's a lot about communion wafers for you. This is the first I'm even hearing of this because I always felt like they made them taste bad on purpose.

2. *If your answers are mostly Bs*—You're a reasonable person with great taste in Americans, but I think you're getting too many penis implants. Or not enough? Go off, Penile King, America is the land of the FREE!

3. *If your answers are mostly Cs*—You're Grimace. And I'm guessing about the replacing your testicles thing that you sat on your testicles at one point? Correct me if I'm wrong, but did you warp your testes by sitting on them and now you want new ones and why not go bigger? Grim! Good luck.

4. *If your answers are mostly Ds*—You seem really cool. Smart and different and not like everyone else in this dumb town. What do you think of my book? I know, ugh, book, it's stupid. I'm not, like, into books or whatever, like . . . you learn so much more from the real world than any "book." I don't even know why I wrote it. Unless you like it?

SPIRITUALITY, DEATH, AND THE AFTERLIFE

"What happens after we die?"

—Dr. Theresa Lawn

One of the most shocking and inevitable facts of life is that it will end. We all will die, and processing this can be extremely difficult. Fear of death is one of the greatest psychological challenges we can face, and in my practice, I see patients who struggle with this fear every day. We're afraid of death because we're unsure of what happens after we die. This is why, for centuries, people have turned to religion for comfort, to help them face whatever lies beyond this life. Could religion help us to put things in perspective? While normally I rely on psychological tools to navigate our human anxieties, perhaps we can learn something about how to process our feelings about death through the lessons that religions teach.

Let's take the famous legend of Jesus Christ for example. Many people derive comfort from this tale. But why? Well, what we know for a fact is that Jesus was the son of God, and perhaps most importantly—he *died for our sins.* Okay. People say that last part all the time, and that makes sense, but my question is: How is him dying for us comforting? To me it's not, because what that means is now when *I* die, I owe him! Big time! Jesus is gonna be waiting for me, because he did me this huge favor (before I was born, and also, I didn't even know him), but now, because of what he did, I *do* owe him. It's really scary to think that when you die, you "cross over" and then you just do a ton of shit for Jesus, whatever he wants, because he died for us, and that's only fair. So, if anything, the whole Jesus story makes me *more* scared of death, because now the afterlife sounds like a lot of work. They say he's nice, but what exactly is Jesus going to make us do?

Well, I can only go on what I've heard, but *they say* that Jesus gets dead people to make him Denver omelettes every morning. Every day. EVERY DAY! And that's his right. He earned them, I'm not saying he didn't!! But I'm scared. I don't know the difference between a Denver omelette and a Western omelette, and if I fuck that up,

Jesus is gonna be so mad. What if . . . what if I get it wrong, and Jesus throws that omelette right back in my face!! And EVERYONE sees!

FUCK, I'M FREAKING RIGHT NOW!!!!!! DEATH IS SO SCARY!!!!

Man, I hate death, and if I've proven anything in this chapter, it's that religion doesn't help, and it might make things worse. I never want to die! It sounds terrible. How can I prepare?

Mostly it's about getting really good at making omelettes. That's the primary way to prepare for death. But on the next page, I do offer one more exercise to help you approach this very difficult topic.

EXERCISE

DEATH

One of the main reasons people are afraid of death is because we do not speak about it. We are so afraid to acknowledge our mortality that we avoid referencing it at all costs. But the truth is: You're going to die and denying it doesn't make it any less real.

For this chapter's exercise, each day, after you've done your daily omelette practice, I'd like you to say: "I am going to die." Say it out loud, as many times as you can. Say it in public, yell it, if possible, with a big smile on your face, making your eyes shine wild with vitality. The important part is showing your acceptance and letting go of resistance, because you're speaking a truth—and of the truth, there can be no fear. Try telling it to your neighbor, to the bus driver, and to the milkman. And then— why not ask the milkman whether *he* is going to die too? If he answers yes, you'll know you've made a friend for life. You'll get free milk too, because you'll be Death Brothers, and a bond will have been formed. I'm sure this will happen.

However . . .

In the unlikely event that the milkman answers that he is *not* going to die—run. I'm telling you, run. If you encounter an undead milkman, my friend, they are DAIRY-FED AND AMERICAN-BRED, they can run at speeds you can't even imagine and they have *trauma*. He will want to punish you for his slow and painful extinction from the American cultural landscape, he will chase you down and consume you, and while it's true that at some point you're going to die, this is not the way you want to go, I promise. Milkmen are highly volatile, they're #DairyStrong and it's been said that dying by a milkman's hand is "udderly terrifying" and that's NOT a joke AT ALL, that's literally how milkmen talk, it's code—everything is udders and ice cream and fat and leche and that's just a beginner's lesson on their dialect, but I'm just saying—you DO NOT want TO DIE THIS WAY!!

Phew! Well, have you normalized death yet? If you haven't, the exercise continues on the next page. There you'll find a game that helps you engage with plain and simple language around death. Today, you can begin to face your own mortality by simply accepting the language around it, and I feel confident that when you see the words on the page, you'll begin to realize that death is, after all, just a natural part of life. Good luck.

WORD SEARCH

DEATH

Search for words below that describe the process of passing away. We're used to avoiding these words, but they are nothing to be afraid of—so do not avoid them here. The more we see the words for what they are—descriptions of a normal human experience—perhaps we can learn to accept them, and in turn, our mortality. I hope this fun game can help you enjoy the life we've been given, by accepting its natural cycle. (Solution on page 139.)

```
W  J  A  K  G  T  O  F  P  S  D  P  W  Z  R  H
L  J  E  U  X  G  O  A  I  A  A  V  A  T  E  E
A  M  I  Y  H  O  R  S  E  M  A  N  D  J  N  A
R  N  H  T  R  F  D  H  F  I  G  E  D  E  O  D
A  U  O  S  L  X  E  G  G  L  C  J  Y  I  I  B
S  R  H  I  I  B  E  H  E  A  D  I  N  G  T  A
K  S  D  E  T  A  T  I  P  A  C  E  D  N  U  S
P  I  E  C  W  A  W  I  J  N  C  O  M  A  C  K
G  U  I  L  L  O  T  I  N  E  O  V  C  M  E  E
B  R  L  D  D  A  T  I  F  D  V  N  D  S  X  T
G  O  L  L  T  A  O  F  P  E  R  R  O  D  E  C
Q  R  U  E  O  P  E  A  X  A  G  R  N  A  P  Q
O  R  A  N  R  R  D  H  A  T  C  E  A  E  G  S
B  E  E  A  C  O  T  W  X  H  I  E  L  H  E  Z
Y  T  E  Z  W  E  T  E  K  S  A  C  D  A  E  H
G  F  R  O  L  L  E  P  O  R  P  C  S  R  L  X
```

BEHEAD	DECAPITATED	HEADBASKET	MCDONALDS
BEHEADING	DECAPITATION	HEADCASKET	PROPELLOR!
BOUNCE	EXECUTIONER	HEADLESS	ROLL
DEATH	FEAR	HORSEMAN	TERROR
DECAPITATE	GUILLOTINE	HEADSMAN	

Reader's Progress: Check-In #2

Now that you are immersed in "the work," how are you finding it? What are some challenges you have faced so far?

_____

_____

_____

_____

_____

Have you been digging deep mentally? What about emotionally?

_____

_____

_____

_____

What is something that you have unearthed?

_____

_____

_____

_____

What does the stuff you unearthed smell like?

_____

_____

_____

_____

Bad smell?

_____

_____

_____

_____

_____

Do you kind of like it though?

_____

_____

_____

_____

_____

Describe the smell more?

_____

_____

_____

_____

_____

In 2011 I broke my arm when I attempted to cartwheel off a moving party bus at BunCon in Puerto Vallarta. When they removed the cast six weeks later, my arm had a smell. To the common nostril, I suppose the smell was "gross," but I personally found it fascinating because of my intellect. I was in awe that the smell was human, and me. Even though I was the one who dealt it, when I smelt it (my arm), the smell made me feel like I was no longer me, that I had transformed, somehow, into a wild animal. I felt powerful, feral, and tangy.

Ha ha—wow, right? Can you even imagine? Dr. Theresa Lawn, "The People's Princess of Redondo" . . . smelling like a wet dog??!![8] We have to laugh. We must laugh! You're required to laugh.

Eventually, of course, I washed my arm and I returned to my normal odor (I have a beautiful and distinct odor—hella distinct). But to this day, I'll never forget the time when Dr. Theresa Lawn went "Beast Mode" (meaning when my arm stunk like seventy-two donkeys in a sauna).

In what way would you say this is your exact experience?

_____

_____

_____

_____

_____

_____

_____

_____

_____

_____

---

[8] A sheepdog drenched in queso.

THE INTERNET, OUR PHONES, AND OUR ATTENTION

"CTWOMMHWTBDTL"

—common texting abbreviation
(Can't Talk Working on My Mental Health with the
Beautiful Dr. Theresa Lawn)

These days, more often than not, we connect with the world through our phones. We peck away on our little screens searching, aching, for connection. We text, we AirDrop, we email, we swipe right, we swipe left, we turn on the flashlight accidentally and then it's just on for days and days, until one morning we blind a man in the Starbucks line with it and he yells at us and we're forced to snatch the egg bite out of his hand and eat it, open-mouthed, our eyes locked with his, in a show of dominance. We hope our phones will bring us together, but can you see how, sometimes, these interactions leave us feeling even further apart? This virtual world we create behind our screens can be very confusing, even dangerous for our mental health.

The word "app" comes from the English word application, and these days, we use them in every area of our lives. We use apps to buy groceries, to play games, to meditate. What's next? Well . . . I've always said that one day there will be an app for going to the bathroom. I've always said that, and I'm saying it again here because if someone makes that app—this is in writing now—it was my idea, and Dr. T-T *will* get her money. Maybe the app is called "Toilitt," and when it's time to go to the bathroom, your phone sends a notification that sounds like a flush? And then somehow the phone is able to process your waste or whatever. Okay, chills . . . I'm really good at this. Eat my ass, Steve Jobs.

Wherever you are.

Rest in Peace, Steven Jobs.

You always were the APPLE . . . of my eye.

As exciting as it can be to think about apps, if we are not careful, they can cause more trouble than they're worth, especially when there is a real human being reaching out to us on the other side. It can be hard to tell the difference between a real emotion and a cyber one. Relationships can feel real, even when they are not. No one is immune to their power. Absolutely no one. Not even the greatest person in the world.

Now, I'm going to share a story about the power of apps to warp our minds, how they can distance us from those we love the most, and the importance of staying grounded in the present.

At 5:17 p.m. last Tuesday, I placed an order with Domino's Pizza. Tuesday nights are pizza night for me and VJ. We eat pizza and watch a pizza-related film, like *Mystic Pizza* or *Licorice Pizza* or *Extremely Loud and Incredibly Pizza*. I ordered two large cheese pizzas with a pint of ranch. I didn't get the Chocolate Lava Crunch Cakes, because I eat clean, and my body is a temple. After placing the order, I activated the door to VJ's chamber, which hissed as it opened, letting out its cryo-steam—but just at that moment, I heard my phone buzz. My phone will do that to get my attention, when it would like me "to have a wee bit of a look," as they say in England. I picked up my phone and I saw something on the screen.

I looked to find a notification from the Domino's app. Since I'm game and cool, I clicked open, deciding to enter the virtual world, and connect with whatever shadowy figure lay within.

"We're firing it up: Mike T. has placed your order in the oven."

What? A . . . person? I laughed. Mike T.? Why did I feel so strange?! Why was I blushing? I laughed again, this time merrily shaking my long, chestnut-colored hair. I typically laugh and shake my hair to indicate to anyone watching that I haven't a care in the world, and also to make sure there are no spiders in it. No spiders came out, so I must have looked very carefree—but my mind drifted back to the notification. Mike T.? I'm not used to meeting people this way, and certainly not "the man behind the pizza." Maybe this app WAS going to increase human connection after all. *Well, nice to meet you, Mike T.*, I thought. *I'm Teresa L. and I'm really flattered that you are taking on "The Theresa Lawn Pizza Project," as it were, and* . . . Wait. Was this just a new friend, I wondered? It was beginning to feel different. "Mike T." Was Mike short for Michael . . . or Micycle? And what of "T"! Now my mind was going wild, what if "T" was for Testicle, what if his name was Micycle Testicle and what if I loved him—

VJ emerged from his chamber and approached me. He flopped his body down on the couch, leaving his customary oil stains everywhere. He clicked on the television, and then did the thing where you burp softly while keeping your mouth closed and the force of the burp sort of puffs out your cheeks. "Pizza," he stated, with his signature flat affect. VJ craved connection, I could tell. My mind was elsewhere, but I tried to make conversation.

"Pizza's on its way!" I said, brightly. "And . . . how are . . . how are your buns, V?"

VJ answered that his buns seemed well, we addressed their firmness, we briefly touched on a new oil he was trying—typical bun chat. But in my head, I kept thinking of the new man in my life, Mike T.

BUZZ, sounded the app.

"Perfection check complete: Mike T. double-checked your order for perfection."

"Perfection." Did it really say that? I hid my phone. Even though VJ quit reading years ago, what if somehow he saw the name Mike T. on the screen and it sent him into a rage? "Perfection," it said. I had goosebumps, because I know the word perfection well—it's what I offer daily—but no man has ever been able to give *me* that gift, and now, this is what Mr. Mike Testicle is offering me? I looked at VJ. He was great and all, but was he perfect? For years, I've settled for men who have full asses, but could it be that they *half-ass* . . . love? Mike T., yes, thank you for giving me perfection, thank you for making me believe I deserve it—

BUZZ.

"We're on the way: Garth left the store with your order at 5:47."

Garth? Who the hell is Garth? What happened to Mike T.! Garth?! Who are you . . . fucking Garth Brooks? God, that seems unlikely.

However.

If that's the case, sir, you're gonna meet "a friend in low places" soon: My <u>foot</u> in your <u>ass</u>. And *GOODBYE* to Mike T. I'm glad you're gone. It wouldn't have worked anyway—you clearly have mommy issues, daddy issues, and you're-gonna-need-some-tissues, 'cause you'll be crying over me for a long-ass time.

Long asses . . . I looked back at VJ. My Vanceony. There he was, my lover, next to me, in flesh and blood, staring blankly at the ad for Cellino and Barnes on the screen. He sang along to the jingle softly, getting every word wrong, even though most of the song is "Cellino and Barnes." I took a moment to watch him. Was *this* not perfection? I asked myself. I knew that it was. I'm perfect, VJ is perfect, my life is perfect, and I want for nothing. Just then, the doorbell rang. And a small voice inside of me guided me to the truth.

"Get the door." The Voice said. "It's Domino's."

Sometimes, I hear that voice—the voice of God—and it grounds me, when I've been lost in distraction and nonsense, like I was with the app. The truest path to spiritual and mental wellness is to unplug, disconnect from our phones, and just <u>be</u>, existing in the present moment and listening to the truth within. "Eat fresh," God continued. "Live más and you must taste the rainbow." And that is what I wish for all of you.

On the next page, you will find an exercise that will hopefully guide you toward a new freedom as you learn how to disconnect from all of the technology we're *told* that we need.

UNPLUG

For the following exercise, I'd like you to disconnect from the virtual world, and reconnect with the actual world by **unplugging**. When was the last time you unplugged? Be honest. Have you just been "running" for . . . weeks? "Powered up" . . . for months? When did we decide that we needed to be plugged in all the time? Do you even *remember* purchasing the bright orange industrial power cord that's coming out of your ass and plugged directly into a wall socket? I bet when you got it, you said, "I'll just use it occasionally to feel connected." Well, how is *that* going, may I ask? I invite you, I implore you, to unplug.

"But, Dr. Theresa, I like the way it feels—"

Of course you do. They WANT it to feel good when we're plugged in. That's why we did it in the first place! It's addictive. However, when we remove the power cord that we store coiled between our butt cheeks, *that's* when we learn to enjoy the real, actual world that surrounds us.

"But what if when I unplug, something happens—and I miss it!"

Something *will* happen. You'll see the real world. You'll look around you and the world will seem new, colors will seem brighter, and food will taste better. Even walking will become easier, because you removed the electrical equipment from your ass and detached it from the wall. You can go to different rooms now. What's in other rooms? You don't know, because you have a bright orange, four-foot industrial electric cable with one end in your ass and the other in the wall, it keeps you there, and that's your life.

"But all my friends are connected—"

Okay, here's a thought: Unplug, walk over to your friend's house, and visit them in their squalid plug room. Just because *they* want to stay plugged in, doesn't mean you have to. But bring an air freshener 'cause plug rooms smell bad. Don't bring a Glade PlugIn because you KNOW the socket is already "occupied" in that room. You could do a spray, or one of those citronella candles. When I go visit a dead-eyed friend in their squalid plug room, I usually go with a citronella candle because citronella also keeps the bugs at bay—and if you've been plugged in for a while, the bugs are there. Plugbugs: That's plug problems 101. Anyways, once you effectively neutralize the plug room odor, you can talk to your friend face to face, and you'll find it's refreshing. Honest. Real.

"Okay, I'm considering this. But if I unplug . . . what do I do all day?"

Oh, my friend. The world is your oyster! You can do all kinds of things. You could take a bike ride, bring a picnic, find a beautiful spot, and then do some shit on your phone. You'll figure it out. We weren't always plugged in. And there's such beauty in the real world. Get out there and discover it.

DREAMS

"Every dream must be studied as if it were a precious penis."

—Sigmund Freud

Dreams have long been considered powerful tools in the therapeutic process, and the study of dreams is an integral part of any mental health practice. Sigmund Freud, Carl Jung, and Carl's Jung Jr. all analyzed their patients' dreams in an effort to better grasp the issues that plague the unconscious. When we can analyze a dream's meaning, we better understand who we are.

One of Carl Jung's greatest psychoanalytic theories was the idea of the collective unconscious, that is—that people all over the world tend to have similar unconscious desires, tendencies, and even dreams, regardless of race, color, or creed. So, while we may see ourselves as very different on the outside, on the inside we share more than we think—including our dreams.

What are these "common dreams" that we all have? Well, for example, most of us have had some kind of dream where we're sitting down to take a test, and then we find we don't know the answers. This indicates that the person having the dream feels anxious and/or unprepared for some difficult situation they are encountering in their life. This is an "anxiety dream" and it appears in many cultures around the globe. Another common dream is one where we show up to school naked. This dream means you're a slut. It also can indicate that you live for the drama (that you're a slut who lives for the drama).

These so-called "anxiety dreams" and "slut dreams" account for over 90% of the dreams we have, globally. The only other common dream we know of is "Hamburger Man." This is the one where you encounter a giant hamburger that talks. The Hamburger Man dream begins with a giant hamburger rolling toward you at top speed. The hamburger then stops abruptly, inches from your face, and introduces itself. Its name is Rand—Randburger Leathers—and typically, at this point, Rand will tip his bun to you. Rand is a hamburger and a gentleman. Then he will start talking, and you always notice that the sound comes out of his pickles when he talks, which freaks you out a little, but also, you're sorry to say, it turns you on. Rand is a hamburger that talks and he's also the guy at your dry cleaners *and* your first-grade teacher, and at the end of the dream Rand's bun falls off and you both find this incredibly distressing.

Sadly, this is the one universal dream Carl Jung failed to mention, most likely because it was too hard for him to understand. Carl Jung was good, but not *great*. Look: He was fine. He did his best, but at the end of the day, he was just a bald man. I'm happy to help out and pick up the slack—just like I've done time and time again. So I'll say this: While it's important to not be too narrow-minded about dream interpretation, as dreams can mean a number of things, one thing the Hamburger Man dream can mean is you ate the old eggplant parm leftovers from Maggiano's again. I would ask yourself, if you have had this dream . . . *did* you eat the eggplant parm leftovers? Please be rigorously honest with yourself about this. Because Carl Jung is watching. He watches from the collective unconscious, and he knows when you're lying. He knows when you are sleeping, he knows when you're awake, he knows when you've been bad or good—so be good for Carl Jung's sake.

FREE DRAWING EXERCISE

DREAM INTERPRETATION

Reflecting on and interpreting our dreams is a skill we can develop throughout our lifetime, but it requires patience and practice. Sometimes, you may only wake up with a fragment in your memory of a scene, image, or feeling in a dream, but you can start from there. What emotions do the remembered moment bring up in you? Can you see how it might relate to your life, your values, your goals, your struggles? What, if anything, is your subconscious trying to tell you? Try not to take things at face value, and remember that the mind communicates in mysterious **images**. On the following page, draw any recent images or sequences you may remember from your dreams, and write down any interpretations that may come to mind. If you feel unsure where to start, I have drawn the images from a recent dream of my own and added the correct interpretation below it.

FREE DRAWING EXERCISE

DREAM INTERPRETATION

McDONALD'S: PART TWO

Of course we weren't *done* with McDonald's. We're never done with McDonald's. Why? Because McDonald's is never done with us. Consider this chapter "going back for seconds" on all that McDonald's has to offer. There's always more. The amount of things we have to learn from McDonald's is infinite, because McDonald's touches the very core of what it means to be a human being.

"But why is this!?" you scream. "I Chicken McNeed to know!" you hiss.

The answer to that question, of course, can be found in McDonald's origins. Do *you* know the story of the founding of McDonald's? If so, you'll know the following story, and I suggest you bow your head respectfully and mouth along as you read. If you *don't* know the story—well, I hope you don't hold an academic "degree" of any sort, because it would be a lie, since you lack a basic intellectual foundation and you're legally dumb. If this describes you . . . perhaps you'd care to learn and grow! I encourage you to read on.

THE STORY OF McDONALD'S

One night, before the founding of McDonald's restaurants, Ronald McDonald (then Ronald McDonald-Atweiler) stepped into the alley outside of Honk Honk's Clown Club to smoke a cigarette. Ronald had just finished another disastrous clowning show and was deeply disheartened. Absolutely no one liked his clowning style. Ironically, this is a style for which he is now famous, and as we know, at its core it consists of three elements: A. Don't make jokes. B. Mostly wave and smile. C. Do not be comedic. But at this point in his life, Ronald had traveled the country on the clown circuit to zero acclaim, because people weren't ready for a clown who was in no way funny and never attempted to be. The audience would boo him, and one time an audience member even kicked him in his clown balls, but they didn't honk or anything like that. Not even his nose honked—it was just plain. That was Ron's style, but to most of America, all of these things meant he wasn't *really* a clown.[9]

So, on this sad eve long ago, cigarette in hand, tears trembling in his eyes—Ronald was on the brink of quitting clowning altogether. Maybe it was time to grow up. Maybe he should just work with his father at Defense Intelligence after all! Out of desperation, Ronald looked to the heavens, and prayed to Jesus for guidance. What he then saw changed his life forever.

In the night sky Ronald saw a group of stars glowing in the formation of a glowing "M." The famous Golden Arches! Upon seeing this vision, Ronald was overcome with spiritual ecstasy—and he now knew what he had to do. The solution was not to quit clowning, but rather, build a restaurant, which would offer delicious shakes, hamburgers, fries, toys for children, etc.—all things that would lure people to him. Then Ronald could just slip the "non-comedic clown" element in there at the restaurant and technically this would mean that people would be smiling and happy near him, and he could pretend it was because of *him*! This solution guaranteed that Ronald would always have an audience and always have eyes on him, which he needed for his self-esteem—but also, sexually, he needed this.

This is the story of McDonald's restaurants, and in a very real way, the story of humanity itself.

---

[9] What's your favorite Ronald McDonald joke? Mine is how he's mute, and mild, and doesn't do anything, ever, except smile and stand there silently. *Maybe* he waves at you, but don't you dare expect anything else. Are his shoes supposed to be funny? Why? Because they're big and red? That's not comedy. Ronald McDonald has zero personality, he's never been funny, and that's radical, that's art, that's . . . McDonald's.

McDONALD'S

Take a break from the book and go to McDonald's right now. Get whatever your heart desires, and get me extra barbecue sauces and mail them to me. Double bag them. Double bag the sauces. Thx.

WORRY, MINDFULNESS, AND THE BREATH

"What, me worry?
Why—I'm hot and have incredible teeth and striking red hair."

—Alfred E. Neuman, *Mad Magazine*

If you're like most of my patients, you struggle at least a little bit with worry and anxious thoughts. Anxiety is excessive worry and fear about everyday situations, and to truly move toward mental wellness, one must learn how to tame the beast of anxiety.

But how can we do that? Well, all worry and anxiety come out of a fear of things that might happen. But if we practice mindfulness, we no longer live in fear of what might happen—because mindfulness is the mental state achieved by focusing our awareness on the present moment. We no longer worry about what *might* be as we ground ourselves in what *is*.

As we begin to think about mindfulness, I'm reminded of the age-old phrase: "Mind over Matter." I'm reminded of this because VJ just walked through the room wearing short shorts that have the phrase "Mind over Matter" printed on the back. Incidentally, the phrase arches over his buttocks—an area of his body that I don't think I've mentioned before, but I do think is worth noting. I had these shorts custom-made for VJ to encourage him to learn about mindfulness, and to stay present and grounded, and while they fit him so tightly that the fabric is strained to its very limit and the lettering is basically cracking off—the message remains clear. If we can understand our minds, we can do anything. Mindfulness encourages us to understand—and even make friends with—our own minds.

So, let's now try *ourselves* to practice mindfulness. Where should we start? Well, one of the simplest ways to do this is breath work, and in the following exercise, I will teach it to you.

BREATH WORK

To practice mindfulness, we can begin with breath work. Breath work simply means breathing deeply while focusing your attention on the breath as we inhale and exhale. When we focus on the breath, we focus less on anxiety, and we learn to be rooted more deeply in our bodies. There's a certain part of VJ's body, by the way, that *I* would like to be deeply rooted in, but I actually didn't mean to write that.

I'd like to now demonstrate breath work by showing how my attention can successfully move away from anxiety, and onto the simple, relaxing, grounding rhythm of my breath.

We'll start with an <u>Initial Anxiety</u>:

"What if VJ's butt shape changed in some way and I found myself unable to cope."

Okay, I'm keenly aware of that anxiety, and so now . . . I breathe.

I *inhale* for four seconds.
I *hold* for seven seconds.
I *exhale* for eight seconds.
All the while, I'm focusing on the breath.

Ahhhh. There we go. And just like that, I'm feeling much better, because now I'm focused on my breath, which smells like Banana Runts. This is part two of breath work. Make your breath smell like Banana Runts and you won't be able to think about anything else. The smell of Banana Runts is interesting, modern, complex— and it's also my signature scent.

One amazing thing I've noticed about breath work is that you can practice it anywhere. Last week, when I was walking through the primate house at the zoo (which I do weekly to inspire the primates to evolve), I exhaled a dense cloud of Banana Runt and the chimps and orangutans began to jump up and down. One whiff of Banana Runts and primates are sent on a beautiful trip down memory lane where they're reminded of "Grandma's home cooking." This scent grounds and relaxes them, because every primate has that one grandma that makes incredible bananas, and no matter how far they go from home or how famous they get—they're still that little primate kid who wants his grandma to make him a hot banana.

Breathe in the beauty of this day and all days, and let it lead you to a place of deep calm. Now, I leave you with a piece of visual art to reflect upon as you try your hand now at breath work.

FOCUSING OUR ATTENTION

Once we have achieved mindfulness, our mind is so very full. Now the question is: What will you do with this newfound fullness? What are you gonna do with all that junk, all that junk inside your

. . . mind trunk?

My thing is, I want to get you drunk off my therapeutic hump—and I want you to understand that you are now so much more powerful because you are finally living fully in the present and you see things as they really are. Let's take advantage of your mental clarity! For the next exercise, I'd like you to use the presence and awareness you gained from your breath work and turn your keen observational skills on the two pictures on the next page. When we're distracted, things seem simple, and the two images might appear to be identical, but they are, in fact, different, and with your new sense of clarity, you may be able to see this. Take the time to study them both and write the differences down as you see them. Sometimes the version of the world we see is edited by our lazy mind—I want you to see the truth of the world around you using your awakened brain. When you see the world, what are you MISSING? What are you IGNORING? What you end up seeing when you really turn your attention on may surprise you.

Reader's Progress: Check-In #3

At this point in your journey, you should have noticed some changes to your mental health. Describe one of the changes below:

_____

_____

_____

_____

In what ways would you say you have grown?

_____

_____

_____

_____

Are you surprised by any areas of growth?

_____

_____

_____

_____

Do you think it's true that we continue to grow all our lives?

_____

_____

_____

_____

_____

How tall are we going to get? I thought we were done.

_____

Okay, well, I'm done. Next question.

NEXT.

I'm not gonna get any taller! I've got slender, nubile bones, I'm not about to push them to their limit, and since I already know how to dunk, what would be the point of being crazy tall anyway?

Oh jeez—look: I don't talk about dunking a lot because when people find out they're like, "Ooh, ooh, Excuse me, Young Miss Pretty, can we hire you on our basketball team?" and right now I don't want to get hired on a basketball team! I've got a lot on my plate, and there's not room on my plate for a basketball, and even if there was room, I know it wouldn't stay on there, because it would roll off.

Aaaaaand, there it is. Is someone *surprised* that the sexy therapist knows how basketballs work? Yeah honey, I know how they work, and if your sorry ass ever had an actual in-person therapy session with me, you'd see I don't use a timer or a clock or whatever, when you're ready to start I just grab a basketball, I start spinning it on my finger, I scream "Y'ALL READY FOR THIS" in your face, you cry about your dad or whatever and when the ball stops spinning, our time is UP, okay? BEEEEEEEEEP. Game over. AIR HORN. "Ladies and gentlemen, youurrrrrrrrrr . . . Minnesota Timberwolves"—I have all of those sounds in my office to indicate the beginning and end of sessions and before you ask, it's not startling, it's invigorating, it IS analysis, and it's how you actually make change.

Ball is LIFE.

. . . Right?

_____

_____

_____

_____

FORGIVENESS

"Forgive me, Father, for I have sinned. It's been one week since you looked at me, cocked your head to the side and said, 'I'm angry.'"

—Barenaked Ladies, confronting their priest at confession

Forgiveness. It's a word that gets thrown around a lot. But words aren't balls, you don't have a mitt, Bo DiMaggio, and Dr. Theresa Lawn did not come to play. So how about we just take a second and talk about what the word "forgiveness" *really* means.

Forgiveness is when we let go of the hurt and resentment that we may feel after feeling victimized by someone. What I tell my patients is that forgiving is a process that is actually more rewarding for the person *forgiving* than the person being *forgiven*. The person who decides to forgive can achieve peace. The person who is being forgiven—maybe not, because they know what they did, and let's hope it forever haunts them.

I have some experience in the matter of forgiveness. This is because . . .

Eleven years ago this July, a guy shushed me in a movie theater and then threw a Junior Mint at me.

That's hard to write. But it is part of my story, and no amount of awards or accolades or Sexiest Therapist Alive covers is going to change that. However, at the end of the day, I realize that I'm *more* than just a victim of someone's cruel sounds or minty rounds. And I find that in practicing forgiveness, I am able to move forward.

But before we get to the forgiveness, it's important you understand the injury.

Twelve years ago on a seemingly normal Tuesday afternoon, I was at a 3:15 p.m. screening of *Cars 2* at the Redondo Beach Regal 14 Cinemas. I love the *Cars* franchise because I consider each of the Cars to be a great American and a true inspiration. I wish I could vote for each of the Cars for mayor, I wish we were related, and also

I wish we shared a beach house together. Ideally, we would go to this beach house one week every summer until ripe old age, and then we would all die together in an explosion. I love the Cars.

So it's understandable then, that when I see each of them arrive on screen, in the movie theater, I stand up and cheer. Those are my guys and we're related! And it's also understandable that when I cheer, I can't cheer in a normal way, because I want the Cars to hear me and understand me—so instead of cheering, I'll beep loudly. Every day for the run of *Cars 2*, I would go to the Redondo Beach Regal Theater 1, and when each Car would arrive on screen, I would stand up and vocally beep to show my appreciation and deep love. And if you are/were worried about my voice getting tired, well, I beep from my diaphragm[10] and am able to beep louder than any car for up to one minute, uninterrupted, so maybe worry less and leave the beeping to me.

One afternoon at the theater, as I began to engage in my powerful beep work, a horrible, bad, hateful man's voice entered my ear:

"Excuse me? Excuse me, ma'am, can you please quiet down?"

I turned to see who would say such an awful remark, and it was a man with a smaller man next to him (who I would later come to realize was a child, and his son). I then stared at the two of them, imagining my eyes were two headlights. "BEEEEEEP": The sound came from my very depths, aimed at father and son.

"Whoa, lady, please stop! Please sit down!"

Of course, I did not sit down! But my bravery came at a cost, because *that's* when I felt it. Something round and hard and minty entered my ear. I screamed louder than

---

[10] Just to be clear, when I say "I beep from my diaphragm," I mean I beep from the dome-shaped muscular partition that separates my thorax from my abdomen. I don't beep from the thin contraceptive device that fits over my cervix, haha. That's where I honk from.

anyone's ever screamed, because I knew I had been shot. Isn't this story so sad? I then ran into the lobby, and I screamed that I was dying. After that, I remember very little.

How does one recover from that? Well, physically, the process was less challenging than you might imagine, because I suffered no medical injuries and in fact, I was in better shape than I'd ever been. Forget about a six-pack—I had a twenty-four-pack, after months of just fucking *working* my core with my beeps. But emotionally—I had been shot. So, the healing process was slow.

After many, many years, I began to realize that holding on to that hate in my heart was hurting me. Not forgiving that evil man and his son—that was only causing *me* stress. I knew deep down that the man would get his punishment from the Devil himself soon enough, after he passed. The Devil, you see, LOVES *Cars*, and he would get why I did what I did and would be appalled at the way I was treated. He's a good guy, the Devil. I've always loved him AND God because I'm not really into binaries like that. I believe in fluidity. In this house, we believe love is love, that science is real, and that I'm Gen Z. Basically, I don't see things like "black" and "white"—there's actually a lot of gray. And brown. I see brown in toilets a lot, but I don't want to talk about that. To even bring that up is gross. Sometimes, it's time to end a chapter when you realize your *reader* wants you to be crasser than you'd like.

Not gonna go there.

FORGIVENESS AND THE ART OF LETTING GO

What are you holding on to? What is it that you can't forgive? Most of us have something in our past, some perceived or real slight, or a painful incident that try as we might, we can't seem to forgive. Maybe someone insulted you when you were a child, and you've never been able to let it go. Maybe a family member deeply hurt your feelings or excluded you in some way.

I hope you'll allow me to hazard a guess about *your* injury. Judging from your specific vibe that you've given off throughout our work in this book, I'm guessing (and correct me if I'm wrong) that in your case a group of teenagers once pointed at you on the subway, laughing, and said: "Yo, ma'am, your diaper is full," because you were wearing harem pants. Am I right? Their words hurt, but you did not let it go. For whatever reason, you then told the teenagers: "Well, if I'm wearing a diaper, I guess it's working for me—I was wearing it last night when I banged all your dads." And maybe *then* a group of middle-aged men across from the teens stood up and said: "Excuse me, we're their fathers—we're all in town for a father-son convention, and last night we were doing an all-male ropes course, so we *didn't* have sex with you." Then maybe, weirdly, the train car clapped at this, which didn't feel awesome, and one guy, like, did a fist pump and said "YESS!"? (Why did they love the dads so much?)

Probably right at this moment, the subway stopped in a station, thank god, and as the doors opened, I bet you turned to the car and said airily: "Well, Dads, it's been real—" and then for SOME REASON—and you'll never be able to understand or comprehend why it had to go this way—it got crazy quiet, and *that* is when you farted so, so, so loud. So loud. Deafening, really. *So* loud that it took a second for it to register that it was a fart, it was so weirdly powerful, the windows actually shook and all the lights came on in the train, and then some alarm was going off (Come ON! Really??) and everyone was gathering around this one old person who I guess thought it was a gunshot (give me a break), and they were like, "Dear me, I'm so scared, dear me, oh no," in this, like, high, old-person voice, and you had to yell "YOU'RE FINE, I FARTED, I JUST FARTED, YOU'RE FINE" in their face a bunch.

Even if that's not exactly right down to every little detail, whatever the situation is that you can't let go of, today, I'd like you to write it down, letting all the painful feelings out, and then I want you to email it to me at DrTheresaLawn@gmail.com. You may release it to me. Let go and let Theresa take whatever it is that you can't forgive. It will be out of your hands at that point. What I do with your email is none of your concern, because you have forgiven the offense, and you have let it go. It wouldn't even matter if I was writing a screenplay and using all the situations as sort of the framework; I'm not going to call it Robert Altman-y or whatever, but kind of like that, where it's about a bunch of weirdos and their issues—everything ties together in the end.

It's time . . . to let go.

SEPARATIONS, FAREWELLS, AND GOODBYES

"Parting is such sweet sorrow.
Really sweet. Parting tastes like Banana Runts."

—William Shakespeare

O h, my dear reader. As you may have guessed, we're nearing the end of our journey together. Now, I know that goodbyes and separation can awaken old wounds. But I have faith that the work you have done will give you all the tools you need to manage this moment. Remember: You're not the same person you were at the beginning of this journey. You are so much stronger now.

Remember the old you? You were so funny. Remember when you bought the book, and you had that crush on me? Remember when you were like, "I'll never change," and you stomped your feet, but then . . . you began to grow? Remember that time you wore the low-rise jeans that you said were "all the rage," and *I* said: "Uh, I don't think I should see your pubis though"? We laughed about it. We got through it! That's what friends do. We support each other and we grow together. My one hope is that you feel lighter now, emotionally, because of the exercises you've done and all that you've learned; you've been able to let go of so much. You used to have such a heaviness about you, and I don't just mean under the eyes. I'm not even talking about your heavy step! I'm saying spiritually you were carrying a lot. Honey . . . and I hope you can hear this in the spirit in which it is intended . . . you had more baggage than Carmen Sandiego!

By the way, while we're talking Carmen, the million-dollar question—"Where in the world is she?"—etc., etc.—come *on*. I feel like she's gotta be in San Diego!! Right? It would just make *sense*, but the thing is, I feel like they never check there. Maybe because San Diego sucks ass. "Where is she?" "Where is she?"—well, probably at some military frat party on the beach or whatever, so I *don't* really care about finding her. However, this reminds me that I *do* want to find Waldo, very much, and I want to know where he is. You know how those books started, right? People forget. They started because Waldo *rolled his grandfather, who was in a wheelchair, into a bonfire*, and then just fucking bolted (people forget this!). Waldo was thinking, I guess, an inheritance would just land in his bank account, and he could just spend the rest of his life "fucking and sucking his way through Ibiza." (Sorry for the language, those are his words from his *disgusting* diaries.)

Well, his plan failed—his grandfather survived, and he's doing great. Honestly, his "plan," if you could even call it that, was so weird! Waldo literally just rolled him in and ran, and his grandfather was just like, "Hey, what?" and rolled himself immediately out, and there were like a ton of people there? He was fine (except the zipper on his pants got super-hot and kind of zinged him, but it was okay). Anyways, Waldo's grandfather is not even behind the *Where's Waldo?* books, he's over it. Mel Gibson (of all people!) heard about the case and funded the books, like: "Where's Waldo, so important, we gotta find him, blah blah blah," and it's like . . . very weird. Like—okay, weird moment of charity from this embattled, fading celebrity, like . . . why is <u>this</u> your cause? It's not gonna make people forget about the other stuff.

Anyways, you digress—point is, Waldo's grandfather, like you, COULD have crumbled under the weight of all the trauma and tragedy in his life. But he's thriving. And I want <u>you</u> to thrive. You have clarity now. You can face your emotions without fear, because you now have the tools to manage whatever may come up. And that's because of the work we did here. I'm so, so proud of you.

This is what it's like to be sane, mentally well, and fully evolved. Enjoy it, cutie. Take that healthy brain out for a spin. You earned it.

A BLESSING FROM
JESUS CHRIST

Hello. I'm a friend of Dr. Lawn's. My name is Jesus, and while I don't typically plug my friends' things or go on their podcasts or whatever, Dr. Theresa Lawn helped me so much that when she asked me to write a concluding blessing for this book, I was more than happy to oblige.

Where to start with Dr. T.! Quite simply: She changed my life. Before I worked with her, I was honestly kind of all over the place, mentally, but I was too shy to talk about it because I'm God, so theoretically I'm "too blessed to be stressed." Thing is, though, I am God, but I *also* am human—that combination is what makes Jesus Jesus. I have, in the past, struggled with human anxieties because they are a part of me. Ultimately, sure: I'm gonna be fine, I'm all-knowing and am overflowing with an infinite amount of universal love. But sometimes, before Dr. Lawn, I would just get in my head, if that makes sense? I had some daddy issues (haha . . . well, I wasn't laughing) and from time to time, I struggled to make sense of my purpose. I died, I went to heaven, I basically had every deceased person in the world making me Denver omelettes, I was meeting really interesting people like Frank Sinatra and Saddam Hussein—I should've been happy, but at the end of every day, I'd be like, okay . . . but . . . why me? I was insecure. Also, I had other weird stuff too, like I was obsessed with keeping my hair long, like I thought I couldn't pull off short hair. My hair looked greasy, and it wasn't—it wasn't that—it was just that I wouldn't cut it. I was afraid.

Anyways, most of the day I'd be in my God headspace, so I wouldn't think about stuff like this, but at night, when I'd try to fall asleep, these anxieties would come up. I couldn't talk to anyone about it, and I didn't know how to process what I was feeling, so what I would do was, I would take these super long drives in my cherry-red Miata, up and down the PCH, just thinking, thinking, thinking, my stringy and dull waist-length hair whipping in the wind. One fall weekend last year, while on one of my drives, I found myself passing through Redondo on the way to a burrito place my cousin had told me about. It was there that I noticed an interesting sign hanging outside of a humble office in a strip mall. "Dr. Theresa Lawn: Therapist," the sign read. In that moment, my God senses kicked in. I can't explain it more than that, basically I saw the sign and was just like: "Yes. I'll have what she's having"—meaning I wanted the healing I knew she offered. So I went inside.

When I entered her office, Dr. Lawn was working at her desk, back turned to me. She was seated atop her exercise ball, tall and shockingly erect. She was typing what I would later find out was the final chapter of this very book. When she turned around to greet me, I saw a flash of recognition, then worry, in her eyes. "It's you," she said softly. "I've always been scared that when I die, you won't like my Denver omelettes." I was about to reassure her with my all-encompassing acceptance and love, but before I could even speak, a determined look came over her face, and without saying a word, Dr. Theresa then rolled across the room on her exercise ball at top speed, directly into the en suite kitchenette. Without so much as looking in my direction, I watched as she began to make an omelette—chopping, dicing, and flipping—all from atop the ball. She was facing her fear. When she finished, she gave the omelette to me and motioned for me to take a bite. I loaded the first forkful into my mouth and . . .

Oh, God.

Reader.

Oh my god! This omelette was so fucking gross!!!!!!!

This omelette was a nightmare, it tasted like shit, and eating it made me feel psychotic. It tasted worse than Hell feels (I think). There was like a lingering fish flavor in there (?), and she put fucking *Reese's Pieces* in it—truly WTF, Theresa. I swallowed that first awful bite and struggled to find anything to say as tension filled the air. But just then . . . something remarkable, entirely unexpected, and nearly miraculous happened. It was as if my palate changed. It evolved. I no longer tasted the ingredients in the omelette—I could no longer taste much of anything aside from the undeniable flavor of innovation. Of courage. Of originality. I had never encountered a mind like Dr. Theresa Lawn's, and, in the end, her omelette was a reflection of her incredible spirit. I love all my children's beautiful, unique spirits.[11] Sure, Dr. Theresa's omelette was a bit of an acquired taste, but bitch, you better <u>believe</u> I acquired it. She had created something very special, and I let her know she had pleased me greatly. This praise addressed her concerns and eased her mind, and thus, we were able to begin our therapeutic work together.

Today, I write you from my summer home in Nantucket, watching as the late afternoon sun dances across the water, seagulls silhouetted against the clouds. A few months ago, Dr. Lawn and I completed our sessions, and I'm happy to report I've now been able to release all my human worries and I've resolved all of my issues thanks to her help and support. I have a buzz cut now. First, I tried pulling all my hair into a high pony, then I did a French braid for a while, but that was all just avoiding what I needed to do, which was cut it off. I did, and now I love the way I look. A buzz cut, I think, flatters my face shape best. It's not like super, super short, it's like a little grown out now, it's not "military" feeling, more just "clean." Sometimes, I'm blown away when I look at myself now because I have these great cheekbones that no one really even saw before. Now they're out, and I look really good. Really, really good.

I look so good.

---

[11] Except people who take karaoke too seriously/only want to sing slow boring songs from *Les Mis*.

All my love and blessings to you, the work you have done here, and to Dr. Theresa Lawn.

Jesus Christ
Nantucket, May 2023

APPENDIX

Chapter 7: Kissing Bob Dole

(Excerpted from On the Dole: An Unexpected Love Story*)*

Sept. 23, 2004, Boise, Idaho

I looked at Bob Dole at the podium, my eyes lingering on his knees. God, I loved his knees. They brought out a horny feeling in me! My mother always told me: "Girls are sugar and spice and everything nice." So how come MISTER Bob Dole was as sweet as sugar, and with kisses as spicy as a Spice Girl! Was *he* a girl? Would my mama think he was? Didn't matter to me—I simply knew I horned for him. As Bob went to greet his supporters, I watched him work the crowd. How I loved to see him in his element. Staring at him, I let my mind wander back to a precious memory of ours—the first time we kissed. It had happened the day before, at a campaign event at the botanical gardens in Twin Falls.

My allergies had been really, really bad that day, but I was mostly brave about it. It was a lovely afternoon, and Bob Dole had just given a speech about taxes and whether he would do them if he became mayor or whatever it was he was doing. He finished speaking and stepped down from the podium and began walking through the crowd, shaking hands. I remember seeing the magnolia trees that lined the edges of the pavilion swaying gently in the breeze. I felt like I was in a movie where me and Bob Dole were the stars, and it was the good kind of movie, the kind where it's just people having sex and that's the movie.

Eventually, Bob Dole arrived in front of me. He extended his hand for a shake, I looked up at him, and that's when I started to sneeze. I've never sneezed so loudly, so many times, and with such vigor. And when I sneeze, I'm quite loud. I grab whoever is standing in front of me to steady myself. Also, I scream when I sneeze, and it's startling. Startling because it's so very loud, but also because it feels aggressive because I'm screaming actual words. So I'll sneeze while saying "RACISM!" or "THE NEW JERSEY TURNPIKE!" or "RACISM!" This time was no different: Bob Dole came up to shake my hand, I sneezed, I held on to his shoulders for dear life, and I screamed. I screamed the words "BOB DOLE." I sneezed approximately thirty times, holding him by the shoulders while screaming his name in a ragged, loud voice directly into his face. It felt like time stopped. Eventually, police officers came over (this is because they had a crush on me). I don't remember what happened next, but it doesn't matter, because a part I forgot to tell you was that I had kissed Bob Dole somewhere in there I think, or I probably did.

Kissing Bob Dole. Wow. Thank you, sir. I'll have another. ;)

```
W J A K G T O F P S D P W Z R H
L J E U X G O A I A A V A T E E
A M I Y H O R S E M A N D J N A
R N H T R F D H F I G E D E O D
A U O S L X E G G L C J Y I I B
S R H I I B E H E A D I N G T A
K S D E T A T I P A C E D N U S
P I E C W A W I J N C O M A C K
G U I L L O T I N E O V C M E E
B R L D D A T I F D V N D S X T
G O L L T A O F P E R R O D E C
Q R U E O P E A X A G R N A P Q
O R A N R R D H A T C E A E G S
B E E A C O T W X H I E L H E Z
Y T E Z W E T E K S A C D A E H
G F R O L L E P O R P C S R L X
```

ACKNOWLEDGMENTS

Special thanks to: Sarah Guzzardo, Kathy Salerno, Max Silvestri, Alex Scordelis, Seth Reiss, Kassia Miller, Pat O'Brien, Alex Rubens, Tiffany Schloesser, Eve Atterman, Allysa Mahler, Amanda Hacohen, Evan Thompson, Charlie Upchurch, my family, and Lionel.

Author Photo: Evan Hoyt Thompson

Emily Altman is an Emmy-nominated writer and performer originally from Philadelphia. She has written for such shows as *Unbreakable Kimmy Schmidt*, *Difficult People*, *The President Show*, and *Inside Amy Schumer* (for which she won a Peabody Award). She has written for *Big Mouth* since its debut season in 2017, where she also serves as co-executive producer and occasional voice actor. Before her comedy writing career, she worked for years as an Italian professor—because she's random like that. She lives in New York City.